The Supply Chain Professional

Concepts and Analytics

F. Robert Jacobs, PhD, Rhonda R. Lummus, PhD

HERCHER PUBLISHING Inc.

Naperville, Illinois

Richard T. Hercher Jr., *Publisher*
Elizabeth Hercher, *Editorial Assistant*
Carol Rose, *Managing Editor*
Jennifer Murtoff, *Editor*
Precision Graphics/Lachina, *Composition*
Courier Companies, Inc., *Printing*

Cover Illustration, Fotolio Inc.

ISBN: 978-1-939297-10-5

This book provides an intensive overview of supply chain management including demand management, and manufacturing and distribution, along with quantitative models used in managing the supply chain.

Supply chain management is the process of planning, implementing, and controlling the efficient, cost-effective flow and storage of raw materials, in-process inventory, finished goods, and related information from point of origin to point of consumption for the purpose of conforming to customer requirements.

The book emphasizes supply chain system design and planning, and provides an introduction to the field of supply chain management through developing an understanding of the managerial issues and challenges of developing and implementing a firm's supply chain strategy. The objective is to familiarize students with the types of decisions involved in designing and controlling material flow in the supply chain system, along with exposing them to a sample of tools available for assisting in making these decisions. The book introduces and applies a number of current concepts (such as supplier partnerships, supply chain strategy, demand planning. etc.) that have significant implications on a firm's competitiveness. Case studies and applications are included to reinforce the concepts.

Students successfully completing a course using this book will achieve the following:

1. Understand the elements of a supply chain management system (including the in- and outbound flows of material and information) and be able to identify the strategic decisions that go into the design, implementation, and modification of such a system;

2. Apply relevant conceptual and analytical tools (especially spreadsheet modeling) that support strategic supply chain design and implementation in a range of areas:

   Supply chain design (mapping and improving supply chains),

   Financial impacts of supply chain decisions,

   Capacity planning, process analysis, and the impact of variability on performance,

   Demand planning (understanding customer demand and forecasting),

   Inventory management (understanding the role of inventory in both a supply chain and a manufacturing environment),

   Managing customer and supplier relationships,

   Supply chain strategy and the role of logistics in supply chains,

   Information exchange in supply chains,

   Supply chain planning and control;

3. Analyze cases with ill-structured supply chain problems and apply sound reasoning in determining appropriate recommendations/action plans.

To aid understanding of the analytic supply chain models, templates have been developed for many of the examples and end-of-chapter problems. The templates are available at http://www.oscm-pro.com/scp/.

The book builds on many concepts from the APICS Body of Knowledge and is a useful reference for those completing the APICS Certified Supply Chain Professional (CSCP) certification.

Contents

Introduction

A **supply chain** is a global network used to deliver goods and services from raw materials to end customers through an engineered flow of information, transformation, physical distribution, and cash. **Supply chain management (SCM)** is the design, planning, execution, control, and monitoring of supply chain activities with the objective of creating net value, building a competitive infrastructure, leveraging worldwide logistics, synchronizing supply with demand, and measuring performance globally.

Supply chain management has become an important managerial issue for a number of reasons. A primary reason stems from increased national and international competition. Customers have multiple sources from which to choose to satisfy demand; therefore, locating product throughout the world for maximum customer accessibility at a minimum cost becomes crucial. Previously, companies looked at solving the distribution problem through maintaining inventory at various locations throughout the chain. However, the dynamic nature of the marketplace makes holding inventory a risky and potentially unprofitable tactic. Customers' buying habits are constantly changing, and competitors are continually adding and deleting products. Demand changes make it almost certain that the company will have the wrong inventory. In addition, most companies cannot provide a low-cost product when funds are tied up in inventory.

Other reasons for emphasis on supply chain management by executives of the company include:

shorter product cycles (increase stock-out risk),

fiercer competition (requires low cost and inventory availability),

technologies that are 'flattening the world' (enables global competition),

trade-offs that are required between departments or functions (assure optimal performance across the company), and

specialization (few companies are vertically integrated).

Managers in companies across the supply chain take an interest in the success of the other companies in their chain. They work together to make the whole supply chain competitive. They have the facts about the market, they know a lot about competition, and they coordinate their activities with those of their trading partners. They use technology to gather information on market demands and exchange information between organizations. These managers also focus on the transportation links between each node within the chain to synchronize the entire supply chain.

SUPPLY CHAINS AND VALUE CREATION

Supply chains create value for the firms that are part of the network. This financial or economic value results from profitably managing the delivery of the company's products and services and returning wealth to shareholders. Supply chains create customer value by delivering a product or service that meets customer requirements. Supply chains can also create social value for the communities where the businesses reside and by minimizing their impact on the environment.

In the context of creating value, a supply chain can be viewed as a **value stream**, which consists of the processes that create, produce, and deliver a good or service to the market. For a good, the value stream encompasses the raw material supplier, the manufacture and assembly of the good, and the distribution network.

One might think of this topic only in the context of producing goods, but it is also useful in service industries. A **service industry**, in its narrowest sense, is an organization that provides an intangible product (e.g., medical or legal advice). In its broadest sense, all organizations except farming, mining, and manufacturing are service industries. This definition of service industry includes retail and wholesale trade; transportation and utilities; finance, insurance, and real estate; construction; professional, personal, and social services; and local, state, and federal governments.

For a service industry, the value stream consists of suppliers, support personnel, technology, the service "producer," and the distribution channel. The value stream may be controlled by a single business or by a network of several businesses.

JOBS IN SUPPLY CHAIN MANAGEMENT

Entry level jobs in supply chain management include the following: buyer/planner, distribution and logistics manager, master scheduling manager, materials manager, and supply chain manager.

The **buyer/planner** is a material buyer who also does material planning. This job manages material acquisition, assists in material requirements planning, supplier relationship management, product life cycle and service design, and other activities related to acquiring resources for a firm.

The **distribution and logistics manager** is responsible for overseeing the flow of goods and related information in the supply chain. This job coordinates supply chain processes that involve suppliers, manufacturers, retailers, and consumers. This role also covers distribution management within logistics, including transportation, warehousing, and monitoring the flow of goods and materials.

The **master scheduling manager** is responsible for managing, establishing, reviewing, and maintaining a master schedule of the need for select items. These managers should have good product, plant, process, and market knowledge since their actions impact customer service, and material and capacity planning.

The **materials manager** supports the complete cycle of material flow, from the purchase and tracking of raw material, tracking of work in process, to the tracking of the finished product, ensuring that material is available to satisfy the demand of customers. The materials manager is responsible for minimizing waste, managing inventory levels, and ensuring that costs are in line with budgets.

The **supply chain manager** is responsible for support of the global network that delivers products and services across the entire supply chain, from raw materials to end customers. With the goal of creating value for the firm and the customer, supply chain managers integrate the design, planning, execution, control, and supervision of supply chain activities. They are responsible for creating a competitive infrastructure that uses worldwide logistics and resources to synchronize supply with demand.

Successful companies clearly define priorities related to the supply chain that will help the supply chain infrastructure be competitive. The following **competitive dimensions** are useful for understanding the basis for developing a supply chain competitive advantage:

Order winners. These are the competitive characteristics that cause a firm's customers to choose that firm's goods and services over those of its competitors. Order winners are competitive advantages for the firm. Order winners usually focus on one (rarely more than two) of the following strategic initiatives: price/cost, quality, delivery speed, delivery reliability, product design, flexibility, after-market service, or image.

Order qualifiers. These are the competitive characteristics that a firm must exhibit to be a viable competitor in the marketplace. For example, a firm may seek to compete on characteristics other than price, but in order to "qualify" to compete, its costs and the related price must be within a certain range to be considered by its customers.

Order losers. These are the capabilities of an organization in which poor performance can cause loss of business. Failure to meet customer expectations with delivery of the product is an order loser.

Integrated resource management is the consistent planning and validation of all organizational resources. It involves effective identification, planning, scheduling, execution, and control of all organizational resources to produce a good or service that provides customer satisfaction and supports the organization's competitive edge and, ultimately, organizational goals. Integrated resource management is a field of study emphasizing the systems perspective, encompassing both the product and process life cycles, and focusing on the integration of organizational resources toward the effective realization of organizational goals. Resources include materials; maintenance, repair, and operating supplies; production and supporting equipment; facilities; direct and indirect employees; staff; administrative and professional employees; information; knowledge; and capital. Key considerations, other than efficiency and cost, are supply chain risk and sustainability.

The concept of **supply chain risk** recognizes that decisions and activities related to designing and operating a supply chain have outcomes that can negatively affect information and goods flows within a supply chain. Disruption of these flows can have a major impact on competitive performance. Global guidelines related to assessing and managing supply chain risk are contained in ISO 31000.

> **ISO 31000 – Risk Management Principles and Guidelines** is a standard adopted by the International Organization for Standardization (ISO) that outlines principles and a set of guidelines to manage risk in any endeavor. The standard includes guidelines for understanding risk, developing a risk management policy, integrating risk management into organizational processes (including accountability and responsibility), and establishing internal and external risk communication processes. ISO 31000 is not a management system standard and is not intended or appropriate for certification purposes or regulatory or contractual use.

Sustainability is an important three-pronged objective in supply chain activities. It is fundamental that all activities should provide benefits today without compromising the needs of future generations. More specific objectives relate to the **financial performance** of the firm, **environmental impact**, and **social responsibility**. Financial performance is addressed in the next chapter. ISO 14000 provides practical tools for companies looking to identify, control and improve their environmental impact. Social responsibility relates to a firm's employee welfare and public policy activities. ISO 26000 provides guidance for how firms should address social responsibility. The following are additional details and noteworthy related global initiatives.

> **ISO 14000 – Environmental Management Systems.** A series of generic environmental management standards developed by the ISO, which provide structure and systems for managing environmental compliance with legislative and regulatory requirements and affect every aspect of a company's environmental operations.

> **ISO 26000 – Guidance for Social Responsibility.** An international standard adopted by the ISO to assist organizations in contributing to sustainable development beyond legal compliance through a common understanding of social responsibility. ISO 26000 is not a management system standard and is not intended or appropriate for certification purposes or regulatory or contractual use.

> **Global Reporting Initiative (GRI).** A network-based organization that pioneered the world's most widely used sustainability reporting framework.

> **United Nations Global Compact.** A voluntary initiative whereby companies embrace, support, and enact, within their sphere of influence, a set of core values in the areas of human rights, labor standards, the environment, and anticorruption.

An important area of supply chain management is logistics. In an industrial context, **logistics** is the art and science of obtaining, producing, and distributing material and products to the proper place and in proper quantities. In a military sense, its meaning can also include the movement of personnel. Due to the highly specialized nature of logistics, many firms use **third-party logistics (3PL)** providers. A 3PL typically involves a buyer and supplier team who work with a third party that provides product delivery services. This third party may provide added supply chain expertise and specialized services.

In addition to the normal flow of goods from supplier to the buying customer, the stream of goods flowing in the opposite direction is also important. **Reverse logistics** is the management of the complete supply chain dedicated to the reverse flow of products and materials for the purpose of returns, repair, remanufacture, and/or recycling. The term **reverse supply chain** refers to items that move from the consumer back to the producer for repair or disposal.

The term **outsourcing** refers to the process of having suppliers provide goods and services that were previously provided internally. Outsourcing involves substitution and potentially the loss of the capability of a previous internal activity.

SUPPLY CHAIN DISCUSSION QUESTIONS

Every year, Gartner, Inc., publishes a report ranking companies with the best supply chain. The Gartner Supply Chain Top 25 comes out in June, followed by reports on specific industries. The Gartner website is: http://www.gartner.com/. Answer the following questions that relate to the Gartner list:

1. How does Gartner determine the rank order?
2. Select a company in the Top 25 and answer the following questions:
   a. What strategies/activities/processes contribute to the company being ranked in the Top 25?
   b. Why would companies want to be included on the list? What can they learn from the company you identified?

STUDY QUESTIONS

The following are unique functions of people in entry-level supply chain management jobs:

   a. purchasing
   b. moving goods
   c. manufacturing plant scheduling
   d. minimizing waste and cost
   e. global material planning

For questions 1 through 5, match the following job titles with the key functions listed above:

1. materials manager _____
2. supply chain manager _____
3. master scheduling manager _____
4. distribution and logistics manager _____
5. buyer/planner _____

6. An organization that provides an intangible product is referred to as a
   a. value stream.
   b. manufacturer.
   c. buying company.
   d. service.
   e. logistics provider.

7. The processes that create, produce, and deliver a good or service to the market are a
   a. distribution channel.
   b. supply chain network.
   c. value stream.
   d. supply map.
   e. market channel.

8. Priorities that relate to how a supply chain is successfully operated are called
   a. competitive dimensions.
   b. risk factors.
   c. qualifiers.
   d. goals.
   e. key performance measures.

9. A capability in which poor performance can result in losing customers is a(n)
   a. order qualifier.
   b. order winner.
   c. product feature.
   d. order loser.
   f. service attribute.

10. A capability that a firm must exhibit to viably compete for business is a(n)
   a. order qualifier.
   b. order winner.
   c. product feature.
   d. order loser.
   e. service attribute.

11. A capability that causes a firm's customers to choose the company is a(n)
   a. order qualifier.
   b. order winner.
   c. product feature.
   d. order loser.
   e. service attribute.

12. A field of study that emphasizes a systems perspective that considers products and processes and their usage over time, the alignment of these products and processes with company goals, and the effective use of all company resources is
  a. supply chain risk management.
  b. material requirements planning.
  c. sustainability.
  d. integrated resource management
  e. ISO 31000.

13. The recognition that the potential impact of disruptions can have a major impact on the competitive performance of a company is the basis for this concept.
  a. supply chain risk management
  b. sustainability
  c. disaster recovery management
  d. earthquake monitoring and risk assessment
  e. risk/reward management

14. The importance of sustainability has received worldwide attention and standards have been adopted in ISO 14000 and ISO 26000. ISO 14000 provides guidelines for how a company can improve which of the following?
  a. critical material acquisition
  b. financial performance
  c. environmental impact
  d. social responsibility
  e. hiring practices

15. ISO 26000 provides guidelines for how a company can improve which of the following?
  a. material acquisition
  b. financial performance
  c. environmental impact
  d. social responsibility
  e. hiring practices

16. A company that specializes in product delivery services and other specialized material movement related expertise is called a
  a. reverse logistics provider.
  b. transportation company.
  c. outsourcing partner.
  d. third-party logistics (3PL) provider.
  e. customer trucking company.

17. Which of these refers to the process of hiring suppliers to provide goods and services that were previously done internally?

    a. external sourcing
    b. purchasing
    c. reverse supplying
    d. offshoring
    e. outsourcing

18. Your human resource manager needs to hire three new people to work in the supply chain area. The first position is for a person who will work with the manufacturing group to help schedule the plant and coordinate the materials needed to support the manufacturing process. The second person will be more of a trouble shooter, looking to reduce cost, stay on budget, and minimize waste related to the use of materials. Finally, the third person will focus on the international procurement of materials and distribution of products for the firms. The best titles for these positions would be the following:

    Position 1: _____

    Position 2: _____

    Position 3: _____

Answers: 1 (d), 2 (e), 3 (c), 4 (b), 5 (a), 6 (d), 7 (c), 8 (a), 9 (d), 10 (a), 11 (b), 12 (d), 13 (a), 14 (c), 15 (d), 16 (d), 17 (e), 18 (1. master scheduling manager, 2. materials manager, 3. supply chain manager)

Financial Analysis

2

In the context of supply chain management, **financial analysis** is oriented toward two major areas: (1) investment in the assets that are required to deliver products and services and (2) management of the direct costs related to delivering the products and services of a firm. Assets are items that appear on the balance sheet in the firm's accounting system. Costs are captured in the income statement accounts in the accounting system. The following are definitions of the relevant terms:

The **balance sheet** is a financial statement showing the resources owned, the debts owed, and the owner's share of a company at a given point in time. For purposes of supply chain management, interest is in the assets of the firm.

Current assets is an accounting classification representing the short-term resources owned by a company, including currency on hand, accounts receivable, and inventory.

Accounts receivable is the value of goods shipped or services rendered to a customer on which payment has not yet been received. The account usually includes an allowance for bad debts.

Inventory is the stocks or items used to support production (raw materials and work-in-process items), supporting activities (maintenance, repair, and operating supplies), and customer service (finished goods and spare parts).

Fixed assets are resources, such as equipment and buildings, acquired for use within a company having an estimated useful life of one year or more.

Accounts payable is the value of goods and services acquired for which payment has not yet been made. This is a liability, or something owed by the company.

Owners' equity is the residual claim by the company's owners or shareholders, or both, to the company's assets less its liabilities.

The **income statement** shows the net income (defined in the following section) for a business over a given period of time.

Sales revenue is the income received by a company from sales of its products and/or services.

Cost of goods sold is an accounting classification useful for determining the amount of direct materials, direct labor, and allocated overhead associated with the products sold during a given period of time. Cost of Goods Sold = Labor + Material + Overhead.

Other revenue is the income received by a company from sources other than its products and/or services, such as stock owned in other companies or the sale of other assets.

Other expenses or **general and administrative expenses (G&A)** is the category of "other" expenses on an income statement that includes the costs of general managers, computer systems, research and development, and others.

Net income or **earnings before interest and taxes (EBIT)** is the total amount realized by a firm after expenses but not including interest and taxes. Net Income = Sales Revenue − Cost of Goods Sold + Other Revenue − Other Expenses.

PERFORMANCE MEASUREMENT

Performance measurement relates to tracking the financial performance of the firm over time. For comparison between companies, common definitions are used within the supply chain industry. Measures can be categorized as financial or nonfinancial. Financial measures are based on data captured through an accounting system, and nonfinancial measures are captured by other systems. Many different frameworks are used for organizing these measures.

A **performance measurement system** is used to collect, measure, and compare a measure to a standard for a specific criterion for an operation, item, good, service, business, etc. A performance measurement system consists of a criterion, a standard, and a measure.

A **balanced scorecard** includes financial and operational measurements used to evaluate organizational or supply chain performance. These measures are often referred to as key performance indicators. Measures in the following four areas are typically included: the customer, business processes, financial, and innovation and learning.

A **key performance indicator (KPI)** is a financial or nonfinancial measure, either tactical or strategic, that is linked to specific strategic goals and objectives. KPIs for a goal of satisfying customer demand might include on-time delivery or order-fulfillment lead time.

COMMON FINANCIAL PERFORMANCE MEASURES

A firm's financial measures are reported on a quarterly or annual basis and capture the impact of business decisions. Supply chain decisions impact many of the financial measures that are used by internal and external stakeholders to evaluate the business's performance. The following is a list of measures:

Return on assets (ROA) is net income for the previous 12 months divided by total assets. ROA = Net Income/(Current Assets + Fixed Assets).

Profit margin is defined on a preinterest and tax basis and calculated based on net income expressed as a percent of total sales and other revenue. Profit Margin = Net Income/(Sales Revenue + Other Revenue).

Asset turnover is total sales revenue and other revenue divided by total current and fixed assets. This is a good measure of operating efficiency because it measures the amount of revenue that a firm generates relative to the investments in current and fixed assets. Asset Turnover = (Sales Revenue + Other Revenue)/(Current Assets + Fixed Assets).

Inventory turnover (IT) is cost of goods sold divided by inventory. IT = Cost of Goods Sold/Inventory.

Return on owner's equity (ROE) is a financial measurement of how successful a company is in creating income for the owners of the organization. A comparison of the ROE with the ROA indicates the effectiveness of financial leverage employed by the firm. The measurement is calculated by dividing the net income by average owner's equity. ROE = Net Income/Owners Equity.

Return on investment (ROI) is a relative measure of financial performance that provides a means for comparing various investments by calculating the profits returned during a specified time period. This is defined in a number of ways by different companies. One interpretation that is consistent with supply chain performance analysis is ROI = Net Income/Current Assets.

Cash-to-cash cycle time is an indicator of how efficiently a company manages its assets to improve cash flow. The measure roughly captures the number of days it takes a business to convert a sale into cash. The measure is defined as follows:

Average Daily Sales = Sales Revenue/Days of Sales

Cost of Sales (percent) = Cost of Goods Sold/Sales Revenue

Daily Cost of Sales = Cost of Sales (percent) × Average Daily Sales

Days of Inventory = Inventory/Daily Cost of Sales

Days of Accounts Receivables = Accounts Receivable/Average Daily Sales

Days of Accounts Payable = Accounts Payable/Daily Cost of Sales

Cash-to-Cash Cycle Time = Days of Inventory + Days of Accounts Receivable – Days of Accounts Payable

Example: Cash-to-Cash Cycle Time

A company had annual sales of $24,480,000 based on 360 days of actual sales. At the end of December they wanted to gauge their performance by evaluating their cash-to-cash cycle time. At the end of the month, the accounting department posted that the accounts receivable balance stood at $400,000 and the accounts payable balance at $320,000. They employed 1,250 people at the end of the year. The supply chain group reported $300,000 in raw material inventory at month end, $400,000 in WIP and $100,000 in finished goods that had not been shipped to customer orders. Cost of goods sold for the year was $14,688,000.

What is this company's cash-to-cash cycle time?

Solution

Average Daily Sales = $24,480,000/360 = $68,000

Cost of Sales (percent) = $14,688,000/$24,480,000 = 0.6 (or 60%)

Daily Cost of Sales = 0.6 × $68,000 = $40,800

Inventory = $300,000 + $400,000 + $100,000 = $800,000

Days of Inventory = $800,000/$40,800 = 19.60784

Days of Accounts Receivables = $400,000/$68,000 = 5.882353

Days of Accounts Payable = $320,000/$40,800 = 7.843137

Cash-to-Cash Cycle Time = 19.60784 + 5.882353 − 7.843137 = 17.64706

COMMON NONFINANCIAL PERFORMANCE MEASURES

Lead time is a span of time required to perform a process (or series of operations). In a logistics context, lead time is the time between recognition of the need for an order and the receipt of goods. Individual components of lead time can include order preparation time, queue time, processing time, move or transportation time, and receiving and inspection time.

The lead time for a soft drink for sale at a retail store might include the time it takes to place the order for the drink from a distributor, plus the time it takes the distributor to process the order and pick it off the warehouse shelf, plus the time to package and ship the item and the time to receive the drink at the retail store and place it on the shelf. For items that are not available at the distributor, the lead time could also include the time to manufacture the item and ship it to the customer and may include the time to order raw materials and components from suppliers to produce the item. The **level of service** is a measure (usually expressed as a percentage) of satisfying demand through inventory or by the current production schedule in time to satisfy the customers' requested delivery dates and quantities. In a make-to-stock environment, level of service is sometimes calculated as the percentage of orders picked complete from stock upon receipt of the customer order, the percentage of line items picked complete, or the percentage of total dollar demand picked complete. In make-to-order and design-to-order environments, level of service is the percentage of times the customer-requested or acknowledged date was met by shipping complete product quantities.

BENCHMARKING

Benchmarking occurs when a company compares its costs, products, and services to another company thought to have superior performance. The benchmark target is often a competitor but is not always a firm in the same industry. Seven types of benchmarking can be done including (1) competitive, (2) financial, (3) functional, (4) performance, (5) process, (6) product, and (7) strategic.

A **competitive analysis** is a benchmarking activity focused on comparing the company to a direct competitor. The analysis includes the competitor's strategies, capabilities, prices, and costs.

Supply Chain Operations Reference-Model (SCOR®) is a process-reference model developed and endorsed by the APICS/Supply Chain Council as the cross-industry standard diagnostic tool for supply chain management. The SCOR-model describes the business activities associated with satisfying a customer's demand, which include plan, source, make, deliver, and return. Use of the model includes analyzing the current state of a company's processes and goals, quantifying operational performance, and comparing company performance to benchmark data. SCOR has developed a set of metrics for supply chain performance, and Supply Chain Council members have formed industry groups to collect best practices information that companies can use to evaluate their supply chain performance.

ANALYZING THE IMPACT OF CHANGES

Financial statements can be modeled by using formulas that relate the information in the balance sheet and income statements. Using a spreadsheet that captures the statements in this way allows the quick evaluation of the potential impact of supply chain initiatives on the financial performance of the firm. These data can be invaluable in prioritizing alternative ideas a firm may have for improvements.

Analyzing the financial impact of supply chain initiatives, such as reducing the cost of materials or reducing assets through outsourcing, is a valuable exercise. It allows the firm to evaluate the potential financial impact of a project while the project is being planned.

The overall key performance measure is return on assets (ROA) because it pulls together both the cost and investment aspects of a project. Evaluating the change in ROA by a before and after comparison can be readily done when considering the investment in a new supply chain initiative.

The relationships are easily modeled using a spreadsheet. The equations that would be used in the spreadsheet are as follows:

Cost of Goods Sold = Labor + Material + Overhead

Net Income = Sales Revenue − Cost of Goods Sold + Other Revenue − Other Expenses

Current Assets = Inventory + Accounts Receivables + Cash

Assets = Current Assets + Fixed Assets

Return on Assets (ROA) = Net Income/Assets

Profit Margin = Net Income/(Sales Revenue + Other Revenue)

Asset Turnover = (Sales Revenue + Other Revenue)/(Current Assets + Fixed Assets)

To illustrate how a model can be used to analyze the attractiveness of a supply chain initiative, consider the following **supply chain improvement model**.

SUPPLY CHAIN IMPROVEMENT MODEL

A firm currently has operating expenses and assets as obtained from the past year financial statements (note all $ are in millions):

Labor = $700, Materials = $2,300, Overhead = $800, Other Expenses = $800

Inventory = $500, Receivables = $300, Cash = $300, Fixed Assets = $2,900

Sales Revenue = $5,000, Other Revenue = $10

The firm is considering a project that would reduce materials cost by 5% and lower inventory assets by 4%. What would be the impact on the firm's ROA, profit margin and asset turnover?

Solution

Current situation

Net Income = $5,000 − ($700 + $2,300 + $800) + ($10 − $800) = $410

Return on Assets (ROA) = $410/($500 + $300 + $300 + $2,900) = 10.25%

Profit Margin = $410/($5,000 + $10) = 8.18%

Asset Turnover = ($5,000 + $10)/($500 + $300 + $300 + $2,900) = 1.2525

After completing the project

Materials = $2,300 × (1 − 0.05) = $2,185 (5% reduction in materials)

Inventory = $500 × (1 − 0.04) = $480 (4% reduction in inventory)

New financial results

Net Income = $5,000 − ($700 + $2,185 + $800) + ($10 − $800) = $525

Return on Assets (ROA) = $525/($480 + $300 + $300 + $2,900) = 13.19%

Profit Margin = $525/($5,000 + $10) = 10.48%

Asset Turnover = ($5,000 + $10)/($480 + $300 + $300 + $2,900) = 1.258794

28.05% increase in Net Income = ($525 − $410)/$410

28.69% increase in ROA = (13.19 − 10.25)/10.25

0.5% increase in Asset Turnover = (1.258794 − 1.2525)/1.2525

Note the significant leverage that the reduction in material cost has on return on assets.

FINANCIAL IMPACT PROBLEMS

1) Your firm is reporting the following financial information to its shareholders.

	Current ($M)
Expenses	
Labor	$700
Materials	$2,300
Overhead	$800
Operating Expenses	$3,800
Other Expenses	$800
Assets	
Inventory	$500
Receivables	$300
Cash	$300
Current Assets	$1,100
Fixed Assets	$2,900
Revenue	
Sales Revenue	$5,000
Other Revenue	$10
Performance Measures	
Net Income	$410
Return on Assets (ROA)	10.25%
Profit Margin	8.18%
Asset Turnover	1.2525

Starting with the *Financial Impact Template* spreadsheet available from http://www.oscm-pro.com/scp/, replicate the calculations for net income, return on assets, profit margin, and asset turnover shown in the preceding table.

Modify your spreadsheet so that it is capable of calculating changes in net income, return on assets, profit margin, and asset turnover based on percent changes in the various accounts. In the example in the chapter a reduction of materials by 5% and inventory by 4% results in 28.05% change in net income, a 28.69% change in return on assets, a 28.05% change in profit margin, and a 0.50% change in asset turnover.

Format your spreadsheet like the following:

	A	B	C	D	E	F
1						
2		Current ($M)	Change (%)	New		
3	**Expenses**					
4	Labor	$700.00		$700.00		
5	Materials	$2,300.00	-5%	$2,185.00		
6	Overhead	$800.00		$800.00		
7	Operating Expenses	$3,800.00		$3,685.00		
8						
9	Other Expenses	$800.00		$800.00		
10						
11	**Assets**					
12	Inventory	$500.00	-4%	$480.00		
13	Receivables	$300.00		$300.00		
14	Cash	$300.00		$300.00		
15	Current Assets	$1,100.00		$1,080.00		
16						
17	Fixed Assets	$2,900.00		$2,900.00		
18						
19	**Revenue**					
20	Sales Revenue	$5,000.00		$5,000.00		
21	Other Revenue	$10.00		$10.00		
22						
23	**Performance Measures**				Change	
24	Net Income	$410.00		$525.00	28.05%	
25	Return on Assets (ROA)	10.25%		13.19%	28.69%	
26						
27	Profit Margin	8.18%		10.48%	28.05%	
28	Asset Turnover	1.2525		1.258794	0.50%	
29						

Analysis

a) Starting from the "current" financial data, use your spreadsheet to predict changes in the key performance measures for a project that is predicted to reduce labor by 10% and overhead by 5%.

b) Your firm is considering a project where a major assembly would be outsourced. You estimate that this project would reduce labor cost by 4% but increase material cost by 1%. Further, you expect that you could reduce your fixed assets by about 10%. Starting from the "current" financial data, what would be the impact of this project on your firm's performance measures?

c) If you were given free choice to develop a new project that focuses on any two financial accounts, what would you focus on if your goal was to improve return on assets. (Assume that you could make a 1% improvement in each of these accounts.)

2) Ceramics, Inc. (CI), a company that manufactures bath tiles, is interested in measuring inventory effectiveness. Last year the cost of goods sold at CI was $200,000 on sales of $250,000. The average inventory in dollars was $12,000. At the end of the year, CI had outstanding receivables of $30,000 and payables of $20,000.

a) Calculate the inventory turnover for CI.

b) Calculate the days of inventory. Assume that CI operates 6 days per week and 52 weeks per year.

c) Calculate the weeks of inventory. Assume 52 weeks per year.

d) What is the cash-to-cash cycle time at CI?

Assume it is December 31, and CI has exactly $12,000 in inventory. CI has a forecast of $11,000 in sales for January and $9,000 in February. How many days of forecast can be met with the current inventory given there are 23 work days in January and 21 in February? (Use specifics, not averages.)

STUDY QUESTIONS

1. This is a financial statement showing assets, liabilities and the shareholders ownership of a company.
   a. income statement
   b. current assets
   c. balance sheet
   d. accounts payable
   e. sales revenue

2. This is an accounting classification representing the short-term resources that the company owns.
   a. accounts receivable
   b. inventory
   c. owners' equity
   d. current assets
   e. current liabilities

3. Which of these items are on the income statement?
   a. sales revenue and current assets
   b. general and administrative expenses
   c. net income and owners' equity
   d. earnings before interest and taxes and accounts receivable
   e. fixed assets and accounts payable

4. Which of the following is an example of a performance measurement system?
   a. a balanced scorecard
   b. the balance sheet
   c. the income statement
   d. a company's stock price
   e. cash flow

Consider the following accounting classifications (these will be used in questions 5 through 12):

    a. current assets
    b. fixed assets
    c. liability
    d. owners' equity
    e. cost of goods sold
    f. general and administrative expenses

Categorize the following items into one of these classifications.

5. an invoice from a supplier that has not been paid _____

6. the money that a firm's customers owe the company _____

7. the items stored in a distribution center _____

8. a milling machine owned by a company _____

9. the amount paid to hourly employees working in a manufacturing plant
_____

10. the amount paid to employees working in the corporate accounting department
_____

11. inventory kept by the company to service equipment in the maintenance department _____

12. the salary paid the chief operating officer of the company _____

13. Which of the following approaches to benchmarking could be described as a competitive analysis?
    a. Employees at the firm ignore the way they have always processed customer orders and design an entirely new way to do so.
    b. Employees at the firm visit a supplier to work on a new product design idea, using parts from the supplier.
    c. Employees at the firm purchase a product from a company that makes a similar product and take it apart to get design ideas for their next generation product.
    d. Employees at the firm take classes in quality improvement and make small, incremental changes to their order-filling processes.

Answers: 1 (c), 2 (d), 3 (b), 4 (a), 5 (c), 6 (a), 7 (a), 8 (b), 9 (e), 10 (f), 11 (a), 12 (f), 13 (c)

3

Product Design

The stages a new product goes through from beginning to end (i.e., from introduction through growth, maturity, and decline) are call the **product life cycle**. This includes the time from initial research and development to the time at which sales end and product support is withdrawn. During the product life cycle, a product can be produced and marketed profitably.

Quality function deployment (QFD) is a methodology designed to ensure that all the major requirements of the customer are identified and subsequently met or exceeded through the resulting product design process and the design and operation of the supporting production management system. QFD can be viewed as a set of communication and translation tools. QFD tries to eliminate the gap between what the customer wants in a new product and what the product is capable of delivering. QFD often leads to a clear identification of the major requirements of the customers. These expectations are referred to as the **voice of the customer (VOC)**.

A company seeks to make its products distinct through non-price-based **product differentiation**. This type of strategy distinguishes the product on features such as availability, durability, quality, or reliability.

Products are often designed to meet a specific price point to be competitive with similar products. The process of designing a product to meet a specific cost objective is called target costing. **Target costing** involves setting the planned selling price, subtracting the desired profit as well as marketing and distribution costs, thus leaving the required manufacturing or target cost.

Enhancement of a firm's product design in consideration of the issues that will arise in the overall supply chain—from raw material to the final stage of the product's life cycle is called **design for the supply chain**. The **total cost of ownership (TCO)** for a product is the sum of all the costs associated with every activity of the supply stream related to the product including its initial cost, maintenance, and eventual disposal. The main insight that TCO offers to the supply chain manager is the understanding that the acquisition cost is often a very small portion of the total cost of ownership.

Products sold into different markets are designed with consideration of the specialized needs of the market. **Universality** is when an existing design of a product currently sold in a single market is extended so that it can be sold in other markets. **Glocalization** is a combination of "globalization" and "localization" and refers to a form of postponement where a product or service is developed for distribution globally but is modified to meet the needs of a local market. The modifications are made to conform to local laws, customs, culture, or preferences.

Postponement is the process of delaying product customization until the product is closer to the customer. For example, a manufacturer of dishwashers produces and ships the dishwasher without the different colored doors attached. Inventories of the different colored doors are maintained at the distribution centers. When orders arrive, the right colored doors can be attached quickly and the units shipped, reducing inventory requirements.

A **product family** is a group of products with similar characteristics from a product and/or sales view. Often planning is greatly simplified by aggregating demand to the product family level. A product family is designed using a **modular design strategy** where common components or subassemblies can be used in current and future products. Automobiles and personal computers are examples of modular designs.

To ensure that the firm can provide products or services that meet Six Sigma quality levels, a **design for Six Sigma** approach is pursued. These quality levels correspond to approximately 3.4 defects per million opportunities. This will be discussed in Chapter 4.

Products that can no longer be produced profitably are evaluated for possible elimination or replacement.

End-of-life management is performed with an old product prior to its replacement becoming available. The purpose is to avoid having excessive inventory and an out-of-stock situation prior to the product becoming obsolete.

Obsolescence is the condition of a product being out of date. Typically there is a significant loss of value at this time due to the development of new, possibly more useful and more economical methods, processes, or machinery.

PRODUCT COST PROBLEMS

1) A buyer for a frozen yogurt franchise with 145 stores is responsible for all the asset purchases at her company. She has decided to upgrade the equipment of her outlets by installing new cash registers. She believes that if she purchases these latest cash registers, they will last for the next eight years. She is considering a quote from a supplier who agreed to supply the cash registers for $1,050 per register. The buyer wants to order one register for each store (145 registers). Along with the registers, she also decided to buy two add-ons for each register—a credit card machine and an automatic coin dispenser. The two accessories would cost her an additional $120 and $185 per register.

As with any purchase of new equipment, support would be required to maintain the equipment. The buyer decided to purchase an eight-year warranty, which would cost $200 per register. She also estimated that she will need to spend money to link the registers to the computer system, which would cost $110 per quarter per register and an additional $160 every six months per register for maintenance. The buyer will need to pay a one-time upfront training charge of $100 per register to train the outlet managers. She also considered the cost of downtime every year (when the registers are not working and another form of cashing people out must be used). She estimated the downtime to be 12 hours per register per year, and the cost to be $55 per hour. She was confident that the high-end registers would have a salvage value of $120 per register at the end of their life.

As she was calculating the cost, she suddenly realized that there were other costs related to the purchase. The cost to install the registers was $380 per register. She calculated that finalizing the sourcing contract for the registers, security service, and other costs would take the work of 2 full-time equivalent people working in the purchasing department exactly 30 days of each person's time. She thought that she would need the help of a sourcing manager who makes a total salary of $160,000 per year and an assistant who earns $105,000 per year. They would place an initial purchase order, which would cost the company $275 and each year they would submit 6 invoices at an estimate of $53 each for the register service costs.

a) Using the data provided above, calculate the total cost of ownership for the buyer's decision (do not consider the time value of money).

b) Where should the buyer focus her efforts to reduce the TCO?

2) You are a buyer for Clinique Corporation, which is considering adding a new lens to their product line of digital cameras. A Dutch supplier produces these lenses and you are considering buying them from that company. The supplier wants to bid on your order. You told him that your demand would be 23,000 units, 36,000 units, 58,000 units and 76,000 units in years 1, 2, 3, and 4, respectively, and he has offered you a competitive price of $80 per unit. As you think through the offer, you also anticipate that the shipping charges would be $3.25 per unit and import/custom charges would be $7.50 per unit. In addition to these costs, there would also be administrative costs, which would amount to $4,200 per month to purchase the lenses.

As an alternative, you can produce the lenses at your own factory, but there are some costs associated with this option as well. Raw materials would cost $23 per unit. Direct labor would cost $21.50 per unit, with an additional 25% surcharge for benefits. Indirect labor is estimated at $17 per unit, plus 25% for benefits. You will also need to purchase a new machine immediately, which will cost $3,000,000 and spend an upfront cost of $800,000 for engineering and design. You plan to add overhead costs at a rate of 60% of the cost of direct labor (not including benefits).

a) What are the costs associated with each of the two options (do not consider the time value of money)?

b) What would be a good option for you?

c) What other issues might you consider when making your decision?

STUDY QUESTIONS

1. A manufacturer of paint uses a system where colors are mixed at the time of customer purchase to the exact color wanted.
   a. This is an example of unused manufacturing capability.
   b. This illustrates the concept of postponement.
   c. This results in extra costs for the manufacturer.
   d. This is an example of the bullwhip effect.

2. Companies who incorporate modular design in the development of new products are
   a. using a team approach to designing the product, with people in different functions.
   b. designing products in a step-by-step fashion, one section at a time.
   c. focused on design for purchasing that considers the current supply base.
   d. increasing customer flexibility by designing products in easily segmented markets.
   e. designing products with components that can be easily incorporated into different products.

3. A fast food restaurant uses only 7 ingredients but offers 15 different hamburgers. This results from the process known as
   a. computer-aided design.
   b. supply chain design.
   c. modular design.
   d. customer design.
   e. service design.

Answers: 1 (b), 2 (e), 3 (c)

Product Quality and Process Improvement

TOTAL QUALITY MANAGEMENT

Total quality is a management philosophy that centers on a set of concepts that relate to how a product or service is made and delivered. The philosophy is centered on producing with minimal defects and continuously improving the process over time in a manner that reduces cost. This cost is referred to as the **cost of quality** and relates to the costs incurred with providing poor quality products or services. Three major concepts related to total quality management are Six Sigma quality, the Define-Measure-Analyze-Improve-Control (DMAIC) process improvement cycle, and just-in-time (JIT) (or lean) manufacturing.

The **Six Sigma Quality** approach is a set of concepts and practices that key on reducing variability in processes and reducing deficiencies in the product. Important elements are (1) producing only 3.4 defects for every one million opportunities or operations; (2) process improvement initiatives striving for Six Sigma–level performance. Six Sigma is a business process that permits organizations to improve bottom-line performance, creating and monitoring business activities to reduce waste and resource requirements while increasing customer satisfaction.

Define-Measure-Analyze-Improve-Control (DMAIC) is a Six Sigma improvement process comprised of five stages: (1) Determine the nature of the problem, (2) Measure existing performance and commence recording data and facts that offer information about the underlying causes of the problem, (3) Study the information to determine the root causes of the problem, (4) Improve the process by effecting solutions to the problem, and (5) Monitor the process until the solutions become ingrained.

Just-in-time (JIT) or **lean manufacturing** is a philosophy of manufacturing based on planned elimination of all waste and on continuous improvement of productivity. It encompasses the successful execution of all manufacturing activities required to produce a final product, from design engineering to delivery, and includes all stages of conversion from raw material onward. The primary elements of just-in-time are to have only the required inventory when needed; improve quality to zero defects; reduce lead times by reducing setup times, queue lengths, and lot sizes; incrementally revise the operations themselves; and accomplish these activities at minimum cost. In the broad sense, it applies to all forms of manufacturing.

PROCESS IMPROVEMENT

A **process** is a chain of logical connected repetitive activities that utilize the enterprise's resources to refine or transform inputs for the purpose of achieving specified and measurable outputs for internal or external customers. Examples of processes include developing new products, identifying new customers, procuring material, planning production, manufacturing, selling, processing customers' orders, providing customer service, researching products, and managing inbound and outbound logistics. Supply chain processes often cross business boundaries.

Business process management (BPM) is a term used when a business discipline or function uses business practices, techniques, and methods to create and improve business processes. BPM is a holistic approach using appropriate process-related business disciplines to gain performance improvements across the enterprise or supply chain. It promotes effectiveness and efficiency while striving for innovation, flexibility, and integration with technology. Most process improvement disciplines or activities can be considered as BPM.

Kaizen is the Japanese term for improvement. It includes the notion of continuous improvement and also the idea of involving those directly responsible for the process in the improvement project. A **kaizen event** is a structured set of activities, carried out by a team of employees, for example, workers in a manufacturing cell, during which improvements are implemented. These activities are carried out over a limited interval of time. A week is typical. The kaizen event is used to quickly implement improvements to a process.

Processes are analyzed using a tool called **value-stream mapping**. Value-stream mapping involves drawing a **process chart** that represents the sequence of work in a process. It serves as a basis for examining and possibly improving the way the work is carried out. The idea is to identify improvements and then document them with a drawing that depicts the most effective process flow. The term **process map** is used to describe a process chart that is constructed using standardized symbols to designate processing steps, flow directions, branching decisions, input and outputs, and other aspects of the process.

Key to the success of value-stream mapping is the identification of value-added and non-value-added process activities. From a conventional accounting view, a **value-added activity** involves the addition of direct labor, direct material, and allocated overhead as assigned at an operation. It is the cost roll-up as a part goes through a manufacturing process to finished inventory. From a value-stream mapping perspective, a value-added activity is one that actually increases the utility of the part from the viewpoint of the customer as it is transformed from raw material to finished inventory. It is the contribution made by a processing step to the final usefulness and value of a product, as seen by the customer. The objective is to eliminate all non-value-added activities in producing and providing a good or service. These non-value-added activities are often referred to as **waste**. In a value-stream mapping sense, waste is any activity that does not add value to the good or service in the eyes of the consumer. Waste might also be the by-product of a process with unique characteristics that may require special management attention due to the pollution or hazard created. Waste production can usually be planned and somewhat controlled. Scrap is another type of waste and is output from a process that is not fit for use by a customer due to quality or other issues.

The **value chain** is a series of functions within a company that add value to the goods or services that the organization sells to customers and for which it receives payment. Closely related is the term **value-chain analysis**, which has been used to capture the bigger supply chain view, rather than a local process view. Using the same mapping tools as value-stream mapping, this analysis creates a timeline that summarizes and examines all links a company uses to produce and deliver its products and services, and depicts what happens to the product from the purchase of raw material to the shipment of finished goods to the customer. The timeline is made up of alternating value-adding times and queuing times, or wait time. An example of a value-chain map is shown here.

Value-chain map

Total Lead Time = 68 days plus 15 minutes
Value Added Time = 15 minutes

The diagram depicts a supply chain for a manufacturing firm. The firm obtains raw material from two suppliers. These materials are fed to a four-step manufacturing process where the product is fabricated using milling, welding, painting, and assembly and inspection. The milling, welding, and painting operations have environmental hazardous storage (EHS) areas. Data given for each process is the cycle time (C/T) which is the time to produce each part, the changeover time (C/O) which is the setup time when a new batch is processed, the uptime which is the percent of time the process is making parts, and the amount of hazardous waste generated each day. Following production, the product is shipped to two customers. This system is managed using a centralized production control system with linkages to all the entities in the supply chain.

The value-stream map indicates that the total lead time for an item produced by the process is 68 days plus 15 minutes, which is the time a unit of raw material enters the system and then exits the system as part of a unit delivered to a customer. Of this total lead time, 15 minutes is value-added time; the rest of the time is spent in storage (this assumes a first-in–first-out inventory retrieval policy).

The value-stream map clearly indicates where the waiting is located (the inventory buffer areas) in the system and the location of the environmental waste. This graphic depiction of the process is an excellent tool to aid the identification of potential areas for improvement of this process.

PROCESS MAPPING AND LITTLE'S LAW

Little's law says there is a relationship between the amount of inventory in a process, the **throughput rate**, and the **flow time** of an item running through the process. Inventory here refers to the average number of units in the process over time. The throughput rate is the capacity at which the system operates over time, e.g., 25 units per day. The flow time is the time that it takes a unit to totally flow through the process, e.g., the time from when raw material enters the process until it exits as part of a finished item.

The relationship is

Inventory = Throughput Rate × Flow Time

This relationship holds for a process running at "steady state" which means operating consistently over a long period of time. "Consistently" means that it runs at the same throughput rate over a period of many days. The relationship does not hold for processes that do not operate consistently.

A simplified view of the system depicted in the previous value-stream map would be the following:

Raw Materials Inventory → Milling → Work-In-Process (WIP) → Welding → WIP → Painting → WIP → Assembly and Inspection → Finished Goods Inventory

This view traces the product from raw materials, through the factory, and finally into finished-goods inventory. The value-stream map gives some clues to the throughput rate and flow time through the system. An analysis of the production process (milling, welding, painting, assembly and inspection) shows that the slowest activity is painting and the cycle time for this activity is 7 minutes per unit. The slowest activity in a process is referred to as the **bottleneck** because that activity limits the total capacity of the process.

Given this cycle time of 7 minutes per unit, the capacity of the system can be estimated if the time that the production processes operate per day is known. Let's assume that production is actually producing parts 7 hours per day (the rest of the time might be consumed by change-over and maintenance activities). Given these assumptions about how the process operates, the throughput rate can be estimated as follows:

Throughput Rate = Daily Production Time/Cycle Time

For this system the throughput rate estimate is (7 hours × 60 minutes/hour)/(7 minutes/unit) = 60 units/day.

Another clue from the value-stream map is the total 68-day lead time of the process (to keep this simple, disregard the extra 15 minutes). In the terms of Little's law, the process flow time is 68 days because this is the total time that it takes material to move completely through the process.

Given the throughput rate and the flow time, Little's law can be used to estimate the total amount of inventory in the system by multiplying the two parameters:

Inventory = 60 units/day × 68 days = 4,080 units

One can think of this inventory as aggregate units moving through the process, because the actual form of a "unit" changes as it moves through the process. Even though exact interpretation may be difficult, Little's law is a fundamental relationship that can be used to get a "big picture" analysis of many different types of processes. Insight provided by the analysis is useful in understanding the potential impact of changes to the process.

The relationship can also be useful to estimate flow time or throughput rate, given that both inventory and one of the other two parameters are known. Using algebra

Throughput Rate = Inventory/Flow time

Flow Time = Inventory/ Throughput Rate

LITTLE'S LAW EXAMPLES

Example—Flow Time

You are in line at the automatic car wash. There are 5 cars in front of you, and you notice that the car wash takes 6 minutes to wash each car. How long do you expect to wait in line?

Solution

This takes some special interpretation of the parameters. Here think of "inventory" as the cars that are waiting in line, so there would be 5 units of inventory in front of you. The cycle time for the system is 6 minutes per car, which is a throughput rate of 10 cars/hour. The flow time is the time you will need to wait until your car is washed. The flow time can be estimated as

Flow Time = 5 cars/10 cars/hour = 0.5 hours

Example—Inventory

At a hospital there are, on average, 60 mothers that arrive to deliver babies per day. The mother and children stay at the hospital an average of two days. If there are two beds in each room of the hospital, how many rooms, on average, are occupied in the hospital?

Solution

Here the inventory is interpreted as the mothers staying in the hospital. The throughput rate is 60 births per day, and the flow time is two days. The inventory (mothers) can be estimated as

Inventory = 60 mothers per day × 2 days = 120 mothers

Assuming that all the rooms are doubles, 60 rooms would be occupied on average in the hospital by mothers.

STUDY QUESTIONS

1. A major focus of value-chain analysis is which of the following?
   a. the identification of high profit products
   b. the identification and elimination of waste
   c. getting customer input to determine the lead time for a product
   d. determining the efficiency of a process
   e. improving the quality of a product

2. Little's Law can be stated as
   a. Flow Time × Throughput Rate = Inventory.
   b. Throughput Rate + Inventory = Flow Time.
   c. Throughput Rate/Flow Time = Inventory.
   d. Inventory × Throughput Rate = Flow Time.
   e. None of the above

3. The slowest activity in a process is referred to as the
   a. buffer activity.
   b. low utilization activity.
   c. choke point.
   d. bottleneck.
   e. release point.

4. If a restaurant can process food orders at a rate of 15 per hour, and during its busy period an average of 10 customers are in the restaurant, how long would a customer expect to wait for her order to be served, assuming there is very little variability in the food preparation time?

   Answer: _____ minutes

5. A factory making integrated circuits starts 1,000 of the wafers used in the circuits each day. This start rate has been steady for many months. Management has tracked the work-in-process in the factory and found it to average 45,000 wafers. What is the flow time for a wafer passing through the factory?

Answer: _____ days

6. A retail store expects 200 customers to be shopping at the store during the peak period each day. Of these customers, about 50% will actually make purchases. The store has 5 clerks and about 20 customers are usually waiting to be served in total. How long does a customer usually have to wait in line?

Answer: _____ minutes

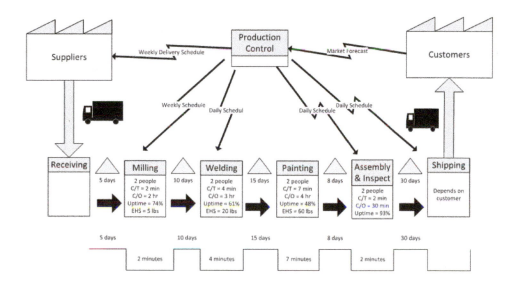

Use the picture above to select the BEST answer to questions 7 and 8:

7. If the milling cycle time (C/T) is reduced to 1.5 minutes and the receiving inventory reduced to 4 days, what are the value-added and non-value-added times for this process?

  a. Value-added time is 9 hours and 30 minutes; non-value-added time is 30 days.

  b. Value-added time is 30 days and 15 minutes; non-value-added time is 63 days.

  c. Value-added time is 13.5 minutes; non-value-added time is 67 days.

  d. Value-added time is 10 people working 40 hours a week; non-value-added time is 33 days.

  e. There is not enough information to answer this question.

8. To reduce the non-value-added time in this process, one suggestion would be to
   a. change assembly and inspection into a process with 4 people, C/O time of 20 minutes, and a total time of 1.5 minutes.
   b. change to shipping by rail, which will cost less and change the shipping time to 35 days.
   c. increase the inventory between painting and assembly and inspection to 10 days to ensure the customer receives full value and never runs out of product.
   d. reduce the C/O time at each process to be 3 hours, in line with welding.
   e. reduce the incoming inventory at receiving to 3 days instead of 5 by eliminating incoming inspection.

9. Jamison Booting, Inc., is looking to implement lean manufacturing. Which of the following outcomes should the company expect if they decide to implement lean manufacturing?
   a. more "just-in-case" extra inventory on the shop floor
   b. more parts and less standardized product configurations
   c. processes that are optimized for their individual purpose
   d. more deliveries from suppliers each week

10. A manager of a process has decided to hold a kaizen event to improve the performance of the process. The manager might use the kaizen event to
   a. calculate standard work times for all employees and design methods to identify those employees who are not working to the new standards.
   b. work on redesigning the process to realign parts of the process into one or more efficient manufacturing cells and reduce the inventory between the cells.
   c. increase the level of inventory to the appropriate amount that will decrease return on investment.
   d. redesign the process to require inspection of 100% of all supplier parts to ensure no defective parts move through the process.

11. The primary reason a process map should be created when improving a process is to
   a. explain to customers all process activity that it takes to make a product so they are knowledgeable about how their item is produced.
   b. satisfy regulatory requirements for all government agencies.
   c. determine what activities must change to accomplish the team objective.
   d. understand the activities, the people performing the activities and performance dimensions of the process.

Answers: 1 (b), 2 (a), 3 (d), 4 ($10/15 \times 60 = 40$ minutes), 5 (45,000 wafers/1,000 wafers/day = 45 days), 6 (20/100/hr = .2 hr or 12 minutes), 7 (c), 8 (e), 9 (d), 10 (b), 11 (d)

Demand Management

Demand is the need for a particular product or component. The demand could come from any number of sources (e.g., a customer order or forecast, an inter-plant requirement, a branch warehouse request for a service part, or the man-ufacturing of another product). At the finished goods level, demand data are usually different from sales data because demand does not necessarily result in sales (i.e., if there is no stock, there will be no sale).

The **demand management process** weighs both customer demand and a firm's output capabilities, and tries to balance the two. **Demand management** is made up of planning, communicating, influencing, and prioritizing demand.

When demand exceeds supply, a firm experiences a shortage or backlog of its product. A buildup of inventory results when supply exceeds demand. Hence, there is a need for forecasting to better predict demand.

When **forecasting demand**, there are generally up to four components of demand: trend, seasonal, cyclical, and random variation. The trend component is the average amount that demand is either increasing or decreasing each period. A seasonal component is the amount that demand changes dependent on the time of the year. A cyclical component is similar to a seasonal component, but does not cycle on a year or calendar basis. The cycle might be very short term, e.g., a few days, or may occur over many years. Random variation is the unpredictable change in demand from what normally occurs.

There are two fundamental approaches to forecasting demand. **Intrinsic forecast methods** predict based on internal factors, such as an average of past sales. These techniques are referred to as **time-series methods** since the pattern in past demand is used to predict future demand. When a definite upward or downward pattern exists, a **trend forecasting model** is used. Trend forecasting models include double exponential smoothing, regression, and triple smoothing.

The second fundamental set of approaches are the **extrinsic forecasting** methods. These methods predict based on one or more correlated leading indicators of demand, such as estimating furniture sales based on housing starts. Extrinsic forecasts tend to be more useful for large aggregations, such as total company sales, than for individual product sales. They are also more appropriate for longer term forecasts, e.g., six months or more in the future.

Forecasting methods are evaluated using measures related to the **forecast error**. The forecast error is the difference between actual demand and forecast demand, and can be stated as an actual deviation (plus or minus), an absolute value or as a percentage of the actual demand. These values would be averaged over a series of forecasts when used as a forecast accuracy measure.

The **demand planning** process uses a combination of quantitatively derived forecasts combined with experience to estimate demand for various items at various points in a supply chain. Several forecasting techniques may be used during the planning process. Often, families of items are aggregated in doing this planning. Aggregation also may occur by geographical region or by life cycle stage.

When there is little actual data available **life cycle analysis** may be used. This quantitative technique uses past patterns of demand data covering the introduction, growth, maturity, saturation, and decline stages of demand of similar products, and applies these patterns to predict demand for a new product or product family.

Firms use the practice of **demand shaping** to influence the demand for a product or service. These practices involve the use of typical marketing strategies such as market segmentation, special pricing incentives, promotion through advertisement, and selecting the location for sales of the product.

Many practitioners today are tapping social media for real-time customer feedback. The idea is to use the information to improve on forecast accuracy. Technology is needed to gather the data, as well as for tools to analyze the flood of demand data to predict the future. **Supply chain analytics** leverages investments in enterprise applications, web technologies, data warehouses, and external data to locate patterns among transactional, demographic, and behavioral data. It combines technology with human effort to identify trends, perform comparisons, and highlight opportunities, even when large amounts of data are available.

DATA ANALYSIS

All forecasts are based on data. A data set is a collection of data. A database is a collection of related files containing records on people, places, or things. A database file is usually organized in a two-dimensional table, where the columns correspond to each individual element of data, and the rows represent records of related data elements.

Data can be categorized in four major ways: categorical, ordinal, interval, and ratio.

Categorical data are sorted according to specified characteristics and involve no particular order or rank relationship, e.g., geographical region (North America, South America, Europe, and Pacific). The categories of data are usually counted or expressed as proportions or percentages.

Ordinal data are ordered or ranked according to some relationship to one another. Ordinal data are more meaningful than categorical data because data can be compared to one another, e.g., rating a service as poor, average, good, very good, or excellent.

Interval data are ordinal and have constant differences between observations. Time of day, for example, is relative to a global location. Calendars have arbitrary starting dates. Differences can be measured with ordinal data.

Ratio data are continuous and have a natural zero. Economic data, such as sales dollars or cost, are ratio data. Statements such as: "This company sold twice as much at half the cost" can be made with ratio data.

Descriptive statistics are used to describe the basic features of data in a study. The frequency distribution and histogram are analysis techniques useful for the analysis of categorical and ordinal data. A **frequency distribution** table shows the number of observations in each category of data. The COUNTIF Excel function is useful for creating this table. A **histogram** is a graphical depiction of a frequency distribution. Frequency distributions and histograms can be created using the *Analysis Toolpak* in Excel. The *Analysis Toolpak* is an Excel add-in that can be accessed from the DATA tab (add it through File → Options → Add-Ins). See Appendix A for additional information on using this tool.

Interval and ratio data can be analyzed statistically. The following are useful descriptive statistical measures:

The **arithmetic mean** is the sum of the observations divided by the number of observations. The Excel AVERAGE function is useful for calculating this.

The **median** is the middle value when the data is sorted from least to greatest. The Excel MEDIAN function is useful for this.

The **range** is the difference between the maximum value and the minimum value in a data set. This can be calculated by subtracting the minimum value from the maximum value (MAX − MIN) in Excel.

The **variance** is a measure of how much the data are spread out from the mean. It is the average of the squared deviations of the observations from the mean. The function VAR.S is used when the data is a sample of all possible values. VAR.P is used when the data capture the entire population (all possible values).

The **standard deviation** is the square root of the variance. The standard deviation is easier to interpret than the variance because its unit of measure is the same as the units of the data. STDEV.S is used for a sample, and STDEV.P is used for the population.

The **standardized value** or **z-score** is a relative measure of the distance of an observation from the arithmetic mean of the sample. The z-score is calculated by subtracting the sample mean from the specific observation and dividing by the sample standard deviation.

The **coefficient of variation (CV)** is a relative measure of the dispersion in data relative to the mean. CV = Standard Deviation/Mean. Lower values correspond to less variation.

The **skewness** or **coefficient of skewness (CS)** measures the degree of asymmetry of observations around the mean. If CS is positive, the distribution of values is positively skewed (i.e., the majority of values are greater than the mean and median). If negative, the distribution is negatively skewed, with the majority of values less than the mean and median. Coefficients between −0.5 and 0.5 indicate relative symmetry. Values between 0.5 and 1 or between −0.5 and −1 represent moderate skewness. The Excel function SKEW calculates the CS.

The **kurtosis** or **coefficient of kurtosis (CK)** refers to the peakedness (high and narrow) or flatness (short and flat topped) of the observations. Distributions with values of CK greater than 3 are more peaked with less dispersion. Distributions with CK values less than −3 are more flat with wide degree of dispersion. The Excel function KURT calculates the CK.

Excel provides a useful tool called *Descriptive Statistics*, which provides the statistical measures described above. This tool is part of the *Analysis Toolpak* in the Excel Data tab.

Another useful tool for understanding a complex data set is *PivotTables*. *PivotTables* is an Excel tool which allows the creation of custom summaries and charts of information in a data set. Data aggregation and cross-tabulations can be quickly accomplished using this tool. See Appendix A for information about using this tool.

DESCRIPTIVE STATISTICS

(Note: This spreadsheet is called *Demand Management Spreadsheet* and is available from http://www.oscm-pro.com/scp/.)

Consider the following data that relate to the sales of suntan lotion at a seaside store:

Week	Sales ($)	Advertising ($)	Average Temperature (°C)
1	669	100	30
2	706	120	27
3	687	105	32
4	699	90	30
5	759	140	32
6	674	100	29
7	677	105	28
8	709	110	32
9	684	90	34
10	678	85	31
11	686	90	32
12	714	100	34
13	718	110	33

The table gives the sales for the first 13 weeks of the year. Also shown is the amount spent for advertising during the week and the average outside air temperature for the week.

Calculate the mean, median, range, variance, standard deviation, and coefficient of variation for sales, advertising, and average temperature.

Week	Sales ($)	Advertising ($)	Average Temperature (°C)
1	669	100	30
2	706	120	27
3	687	105	32
4	699	90	30
5	759	140	32
6	674	100	29
7	677	105	28
8	709	110	32
9	684	90	34
10	678	85	31
11	686	90	32
12	714	100	34
13	718	110	33
Mean (AVERAGE)	696.9231	103.4615385	31.07692
Median (MEDIAN)	687	100	32
Range (MAX–MIN)	90	55	7
Variance (VAR.P)	558.9941	201.4792899	4.378698
Standard Deviation (STDEV.P)	23.64306	14.19434007	2.092534
Coefficient of Variation (STDEV.P/AVERAGE)	0.033925	0.137194365	0.067334

Next, evaluate the shape of the sales, advertising, and average temperature distributions.

Week	Sales ($)	z-Score	Advertising	z-Score	Average Temperature (°C)	z-Score
1	669	−1.18103	100	−0.24387	30	−0.51465
2	706	0.383915	120	1.165145	27	−1.94832
3	687	−0.4197	105	0.108386	32	0.441129
4	699	0.087845	90	−0.94837	30	−0.51465
5	759	2.625588	140	2.574157	32	0.441129
6	674	−0.96955	100	−0.24387	29	−0.99254
7	677	−0.84266	105	0.108386	28	−1.47043
8	709	0.510802	110	0.460639	32	0.441129
9	684	−0.54659	90	−0.94837	34	1.396908

Week	Sales ($)	z-Score	Advertising	z-Score	Average Temperature (°C)	z-Score
10	678	−0.80037	85	−1.30063	31	−0.03676
11	686	−0.462	90	−0.94837	32	0.441129
12	714	0.722281	100	−0.24387	34	1.396908
13	718	0.891464	110	0.460639	33	0.919018
Mean (AVERAGE)	696.9231		103.461538		31.076923	
Standard Deviation (STDEV.P)	23.64306		14.1943401		2.0925339	
Skewness (SKEW.P)	1.182325		1.0795584		-0.404169	
Kurtosis (KURT)	2.231916		2.08078346		-0.558426	

The sales and advertising distributions appear to have positive skewness, meaning there are more values greater than the mean and median. This is indicated by the skewness coefficient being greater than 1. If the value were less than −1, this would indicate more values less than the mean and median. The average temperature does not have this skewness since the measure is between −0.5 and +0.5.

The coefficient of kurtosis is less than 3 and greater than −3, indicating these distributions are fairly normal.

The z-scores are calculated by taking the sales observation minus the mean and dividing by the standard deviation, e.g., for week 1, the z-score = (669 − 696.9321)/23.64306 = −1.18103. This corresponds to a likelihood that approximately 11.8796% of the values are less than or equal to this value. This cumulative probably is calculated using the Excel NORM.S.DIST(z-Score, "TRUE") function.

STATISTICAL DEMAND FORECASTING TECHNIQUES

Intrinsic demand forecasting is where the historic data that is being forecast is used to make the forecast. The most common methods use past demand data of the item to forecast future demand. The **naïve** method is the simplest technique of this type, where the immediate past demand is the forecast for future demand. The following are common intrinsic forecasting models.

Moving averages are an arithmetic average of a certain number (n) of the most recent observations. As each new observation is added, the oldest observation is dropped. The value n (the number of periods to use for the average) reflects responsiveness versus stability in the forecast with a higher value corresponding to less responsiveness and a lower value more responsive. A **weighted moving**

average is similar, but rather than uniformly weighting the past data, weights are assigned according to the importance of each period of past data.

Exponential smoothing is a type of weighted moving average forecasting technique in which past observations are geometrically discounted according to their age. The heaviest weight is assigned to the most recent data. The smoothing is termed *exponential* because data points are weighted in accordance with an exponential function of their age. The technique makes use of a smoothing constant to apply to the difference between the most recent forecast and the current demand data, thus avoiding the necessity of carrying historical demand data. The smoothing constant is a value between 0 and 1, with a higher value corresponding to more responsiveness and a lower value less responsive. Higher-order exponential smoothing models can be used for data with either trend or seasonality or both.

Linear regression is a statistical technique that predicts expected future demand as a linear function of past demand.

Extrinsic demand forecasting uses other categories of data to make the forecast. The most common extrinsic forecasting model uses the regression technique but instead of using past demand data, other data is used in the model. An example of this is given later in the chapter.

Forecast error is evaluated using the following common measures.

Forecast error is the difference between actual demand and forecast demand. This would be a positive value if demand is higher than the forecast or negative if the forecast is higher than demand.

Average forecast error is the average of the forecast error over a set of past forecasts.

Mean absolute deviation (MAD) is the average of the absolute values of the observed forecast errors. This is the average size of the forecast error in units.

Mean absolute percent error (MAPE) is computed by dividing each absolute forecast error by the actual demand, then multiplying by 100 to get the absolute percent error, and computing the average.

Tracking signal is a measure of forecast bias. **Bias** is a consistent forecast error in one direction (high or low). A good forecast is one that is not biased. It is calculated by summing the forecast error over a set of past forecasts and dividing by the MAD.

INTRINSIC DEMAND FORECASTING

The following data are sales from weeks 14 to 26 (the data is in two columns) for the suntan lotion at the seaside store (a continuation of the previous example). Use this data to test the moving average, exponential smoothing, and linear regression intrinsic forecasting techniques. Use the data from weeks 1 to 13 to set the parameters for the techniques, and then test the techniques using the data for weeks 14 to 26. Use the error measures described previously.

Week	Sales ($)		Week	Sales ($)
14	705		21	667
15	699		22	685
16	689		23	690
17	694		24	697
18	706		25	716
19	697		26	695
20	691			

Start by going back to the data for weeks 1 to 13. For the moving average technique, the number of periods to use in the average needs to be determined. For this example, consider using 2, 3, 4 and 5 weeks in the forecast model. Calculate the average error, mean absolute deviation, and mean absolute percent error to evaluate the accuracy of each model. Results are given in the table on page 39.

It is important to understand how these calculations are made. The 5-period moving average forecast is 704.0 = SUM (Week 1 through 5 Sales)/5 = (669 + 706 + 687 + 699 + 759)/5 and is made at the end of Week 5. This number is the forecast for Week 6 Sales, which is 674 units.

The forecast error for the Week 5 forecast is Actual Week 6 Sales − Week 5 Forecast, which is 674 − 704.0 = −30.0.

The percent error for this Week 5 forecast is the absolute error, 30.00, divided by the actual demand expressed as a percent (multiply by 100). In this case (30.0/674) × 100 = 4.5%. In Excel, the cell can be formatted as a percent rather than multiplying by 100.

The sum of the errors is calculated in Excel using the SUM function. The average error is calculated in Excel using the AVERAGE function. Mean absolute deviation is calculated using the AVEDEV function. The tracking signal is the sum of the errors divided by the mean absolute deviation. Finally, the mean absolute percent error is calculated using the AVERAGE function.

It appears that the 3-week moving average model is best compared to the 2, 4 and 5-week models relative to average error and mean absolute deviation. It ties for best relative to the mean absolute percent error. The 3-week Moving Average model is best overall. The Tracking Signal is relatively small, so there is little bias in the forecast.

Moving Average Forecast

Week	Sales	Forecast (weeks)				Forecast Error (weeks)				Percent Error (weeks)			
		2	3	4	5	2	3	4	5	2	3	4	5
1	669												
2	706	687.5											
3	687	696.5	687.3										
4	699	693.0	697.3	690.3									
5	759	729.0	715.0	712.8									
6	674	716.5	710.7	704.8	704.0	-55.0	-41.0	-38.8	-30.0	8.2%	6.1%	5.7%	4.5%
7	677	675.5	703.3	702.3	699.2	-39.5	-33.7	-27.8	-28.0	5.8%	5.0%	4.1%	4.1%
8	709	693.0	686.7	704.8	703.6	33.5	5.7	6.8	9.8	4.7%	0.8%	1.0%	1.4%
9	684	696.5	690.0	686.0	700.6	-9.0	-2.7	-20.8	-19.6	1.3%	0.4%	3.0%	2.9%
10	678	681.0	690.3	687.0	684.4	-18.5	-12.0	-8.0	-22.6	2.7%	1.8%	1.2%	3.3%
11	686	682.0	682.7	689.3	686.8	5.0	-4.3	-1.0	1.6	0.7%	0.6%	0.1%	0.2%
12	714	700.0	692.7	690.5	694.2	32.0	31.3	24.8	27.2	4.5%	4.4%	3.5%	3.8%
13	718	716.0	706.0	699.0	696.0	18.0	25.3	27.5	23.8	2.5%	3.5%	3.8%	3.3%
Sum of the Errors (SUM)						-33.5	-31.3	-37.3	-37.8				
Average Error (AVERAGE)						-4.2	-3.9	-4.7	-4.7				
Mean Absolute Deviation (AVEDEV)						26.3	18.8	19.2	20.3				
Tracking Signal (Sum of Errors/Mean Abs Dev))						-1.3	-1.7	-1.9	-1.9				
Mean Absolute Percent Error (AVERAGE)										3.8%	2.8%	2.8%	2.9%

Next, consider the Exponential Smoothing model. For the simple version of this model, the smoothing constant needs to be found that minimizes the error measures. The following table has the calculations using an Exponential Smoothing model with a smoothing constant of .086.

Exponential Smoothing Forecast

Smoothing Constant		0.086		
Week	Sales	Forecast	Forecast Error	Percent Error
1	669	669.0		
2	706	672.2		
3	687	673.5		
4	699	675.7		
5	759	682.8		
6	674	682.1	-8.8	1.3%
7	677	681.6	-5.1	0.8%
8	709	684.0	27.4	3.9%
9	684	684.0	0.0	0.0%
10	678	683.5	-6.0	0.9%
11	686	683.7	2.5	0.4%
12	714	686.3	30.3	4.2%
13	718	689.0	31.7	4.4%
Sum of the Errors			71.9	
Average Error			9.0	
Mean Absolute Deviation (MAD)			15.6	
Tracking Signal (TS)			4.6	
Mean Absolute Percent Error (MAPE)				2.0%

Notice that for this model, errors are calculated over the same 8 periods (6 through 13) as used in the moving average analysis. For the first forecast in period 2, the previous demand is used. This is done to get the calculations started because previous data are not available. After this the forecasts are made using the exponential smoothing model:

New Forecast = Previous Forecast + Smoothing Constant × (Actual Demand − Previous Forecast)

The week 2 forecast of 670.8 units = 669.0 + 0.086 × (706 − 669.0) is made at the end of week 2 and corresponds to expected demand in week 3 (and the future).

The smoothing constant value of 0.086 is found by using the Excel Solver (see Appendix A for information about using this tool). The objective cell is set to minimize the mean absolute deviation, by changing the smoothing constant cell. Constraints limit the smoothing constant to be less than 1 and greater than 0.

It appears that exponential smoothing is superior to the 3-week moving average model relative to mean absolute deviation and mean absolute percent error. The tracking signal indicates there may be some bias in the forecast.

The last intrinsic demand forecasting technique to set up is the linear regression model (see Appendix A for information about using this tool). This can be quickly done by fitting a linear line to our 13 weeks of sales data. The following chart shows the sales data and a regression line:

Linear Regression Model

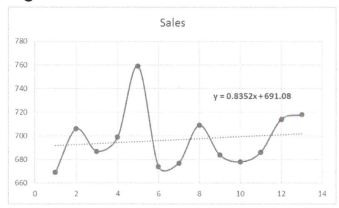

Constant	691.08	Trend	0.8352	
Week	Sales	Forecast	Forecast Error	Percent Error
1	669			
2	706			
3	687			
4	699			
5	759	696.1		
6	674	696.9	−22.1	3.3%
7	677	697.8	−19.9	2.9%
8	709	698.6	11.2	1.6%
9	684	699.4	−14.6	2.1%
10	678	700.3	−21.4	3.2%
11	686	701.1	−14.3	2.1%
12	714	701.9	12.9	1.8%
13	718	702.8	16.1	2.2%
Sum of the Errors			−52.1	
Average Error			−6.5	
Mean Absolute Deviation (AVEDEV)			14.9	
Tracking Signal (Sum of Errors/MAD)			−3.5	
Mean Absolute Percent Error (MAPE)				2.4%

The Week 5 forecast for week 6 demand is calculated using the regression equation

Forecast = 691.08 + 0.8352 × 6 = 696.1 units

Compared to the exponential smoothing forecast, it appears that the linear regression model is better than the exponential smoothing model relative to mean absolute deviation, but not as good relative to mean absolute percent error.

At this point, there are three competing models that can be tested using the data from weeks 14 through 26. The three models are the following:

3-period moving average

Exponential smoothing with a smoothing constant of 0.086

Linear regression model with an intercept of 691.08 and trend of 0.8352

To keep the analysis simple, the mean absolute percent error measure will be used for the final comparison.

Intrinsic Forecasting Model Comparison

Week	Demand	3-Period Moving Average	Percent Error	Exponential Smoothing (Constant = 0.086)	Percent Error	Regression (691.08 + 0.8352 × Week)	Percent Error
11	686						
12	714						
13	718	706.0		689.0		702.8	
14	705	712.3	0.1%	690.4	2.3%	703.6	0.3%
15	699	707.3	1.9%	691.1	1.2%	704.4	0.7%
16	689	697.7	2.7%	690.9	0.3%	705.3	2.2%
17	694	694.0	0.5%	691.2	0.4%	706.1	1.6%
18	706	696.3	1.7%	692.5	2.1%	706.9	0.0%
19	697	699.0	0.1%	692.9	0.6%	707.8	1.4%
20	691	698.0	1.2%	692.7	0.3%	708.6	2.4%
21	667	685.0	4.6%	690.5	3.9%	709.5	5.9%
22	685	681.0	0.0%	690.0	0.8%	710.3	3.4%
23	690	680.7	1.3%	690.0	0.0%	711.1	2.9%
24	697	690.7	2.3%	690.6	1.0%	712.0	2.0%
25	716	701.0	3.5%	692.8	3.5%	712.8	0.6%
26	695	702.7	0.9%	693.0	0.3%	713.6	2.6%
Mean Absolute Percent Error (MAPE)			1.6%		1.3%		2.0%

The comparison is run over the week 14–26 sample that was "held out" for testing the models. Of course, these data could have been used for setting the parameters for the models, but using the sample for testing allows a more real check for what might happen if the models would have been used over this period of time.

Using the "held out" sample shows that the exponential smoothing model slightly outperforms the 3-week moving average and the regression model. All three of these models actually perform fairly well.

For a real world analysis, it would be good to perform a similar analysis of a group of items that are representative of the situation. A model that consistently does well over the entire group can then be selected for actual use.

EXTRINSIC DEMAND FORECASTING

Extrinsic demand forecasting uses categories of data other than actual sales to make forecasts. Returning to the original suntan lotion example from the seaside store, other data that might be used to forecast sales are advertising and average temperature. A regression model is ideal for this analysis.

The analysis will use an approach similar to that used with the intrinsic demand forecasting example. First, the data from weeks 1 through 13 will be used to parameterize the model. The model will then be tested using data from weeks 14 through 26.

The data for periods 1 through 13 are as follows:

Week	Sales ($)	Advertising ($)	Average Temperature (°C)
1	669	100	30
2	706	120	27
3	687	105	32
4	699	90	30
5	759	140	32
6	674	100	29
7	677	105	28
8	709	110	32
9	684	90	34
10	678	85	31
11	686	90	32
12	714	100	34
13	718	110	33

Under *Data Analysis*, select the *Regression* tool. The "Input Y Range" is the Sales range, "Input X Range" is the advertising and average temperature range.

Executing the tool gives the following output:

SUMMARY OUTPUT

Regression Statistics

Multiple R	0.87786443
R Square	0.770645958
Adjusted R Square	0.724775149
Standard Error	12.91006655
Observations	13

ANOVA

	df	SS	MS	F	Significance F
Regression	2	5600.224893	2800.112	16.80036	0.000634647
Residual	10	1666.698184	166.6698		
Total	12	7266.923077			

	Coefficients	Standard Error	t Stat	P-value	Lower 95%	Upper 95%	Lower 95.0%	Upper 95.0%
Intercept	403.3117578	63.10423645	6.391199	7.92E-05	262.7067569	543.9167588	262.7067569	543.9167588
Advertising	1.377641598	0.254709249	5.408683	0.000298	0.810114024	1.945169172	0.810114024	1.945169172
Average Temp	4.861433663	1.727775908	2.813695	0.018358	1.011709035	8.71115829	1.011709035	8.71115829

The result is a linear regression equation that can be used to forecast sales, based on the anticipated advertising budget and expected average temperature each week. The actual equation is circled above and is the following:

Sales = 403.3117578 + 1.377641598 × Advertising + 4.861433663 × Average Temperature

The regression equation appears to be a good "fit." This is indicated by an *R* Square of 0.770645958; the closer to 1.0, the better. The F value is 16.80036, which is very good, with a significance of 0.000634647. Values of F greater than 4 with significance close to 0 are good. The details for fully understanding the statistical data given here can be found in a book that specializes in this type of analysis.

The extrinsic forecasting model is tested using data from periods 14 through 26 presented previously. Here estimates of advertising and expected average temperatures would need to be supplied to use the model.

The forecasts are shown next:

| | Intercept | Coefficients | | | |
| | 403.3117578 | 1.377641598 | 4.861433663 | | |
Week	Sales ($)	Advertising ($)	Average Temperature (°C)	Forecast	Percent Error
13				703.5	
14	705	105	32	720.1	0.2%
15	699	110	34	686.9	3.0%
16	689	100	30	702.7	0.3%
17	694	115	29	710.4	1.3%
18	706	110	32	719.3	0.6%
19	697	120	31	707.6	3.2%
20	691	115	30	686.9	2.4%
21	667	100	30	675.2	3.0%
22	685	95	29	693.8	1.4%
23	690	105	30	710.4	0.6%
24	697	110	32	707.6	1.9%
25	716	115	30	695.8	1.2%
26	695	110	29		0.1%
Mean Absolute Percent Error (MAPE)					1.5%

The forecast for week 14 (made in week 13), for example, is calculated:

703.5 = 403.3117578 + 1.377641598 × 105 + 4.861433663 × 32

This model gives results that are similar to the intrinsic forecasting models with a mean absolute percent error equal to 1.5%.

DESCRIPTIVE STATISTICAL MEASURE PROBLEMS

1) Using the Excel file *Facetime* Survey, do the following (note all Excel files are available from http://www.oscm-pro.com/scp/):

a) Find the average and median hours online/week and number of friends in the sample using the appropriate Excel functions. Compute the range and evaluate skewness and kurtosis measures.

b) Use a PivotTable to find the average and standard deviation of hours online/week and number of friends for females and males in the sample.

2) Using the *Electronic Sales Database*, do the following:

a) Use a PivotTable to find the proportion of customers who used PayPal and the proportion of customers who used credit cards. Within the PayPal and credit card customers, find the proportion that purchased a book and the proportion that purchased a DVD.

b) Use a PivotTable to find the average and standard deviation of sales in the database. Also, find the average sales by source (web or e-mail).

FORECASTING PROBLEMS

1) For the data in the Excel file *Propane Gas Prices* do the following:

a) Develop spreadsheet models for forecasting prices using simple moving average and simple exponential smoothing. So that we can compare our results, first develop a 3-period moving average model and a simple exponential smoothing model with a smoothing constant of 0.3. Use mean absolute deviation (MAD) and mean absolute percent error (MAPE) to evaluate the forecasts made with these models.

b) Using MAD and MAPE as guidance, find the best smoothing constant for exponential smoothing.

c) Using your results from 1a and 1b, what would be the best forecasting model?

2) The data in the Excel file *Memory Chip Data* show the demand for one type of chip used in industrial equipment from a small manufacturer.

a) Construct a line chart of the data. What appears to happen when a new chip is introduced?

b) Develop a causal regression model to forecast demand that includes both time and the introduction of a new chip as explanatory variables.

c) What would the forecast be for the next month if a new chip is introduced? What would it be if a new chip is not introduced?

Zero-Turn Mowing Equipment

The director of marketing at Zero-Turn Mowing Equipment (ZME) wants some detailed statistical analysis about much of the data in the *ZME Database* available at http://www.oscm-pro/scp/. In particular, she wants to know the following:

   a. The mean satisfaction ratings by year and region in the worksheets *Dealer Satisfaction* and *End-User Satisfaction*. How have the ratings changed over time?

   b. A statistical summary for the *Customer Survey Data* by region. At a minimum, calculate the average quality, ease of use, price, and service for each region.

   c. How the response times differ in each quarter of the worksheet *Response Time*. At a minimum, calculate the mean and standard deviation of the response time. How has the response time changed over time?

   d. How defects after delivery (worksheet *Defects after Delivery*) have changed over these 5 years.

   e. Perform these analyses and summarize your results in a short written report to the director of marketing. What would you suggest she focus on over the next year?

STUDY QUESTIONS

   1. A six-month moving average forecast is better than a three-month moving average forecast if demand
      a. is rather stable.
      b. has been changing due to recent promotional efforts.
      c. follows a downward trend.
      d. follows a seasonal pattern that repeats itself twice a year.
      e. follows an upward trend.

   2. Which of the following circumstances would cause a forecaster to consider increasing the size of the smoothing constant α?
      a. The older demand is more representative than the most recent demand.
      b. The most recent demand is more representative than the older past demand.
      c. There is an upward trend in the data.
      d. There is a downward trend in the data.
      e. Demand is expected to remain very stable.

3. For a given product demand, the times series trend equation is $25.3 + 2.1x$. What is your forecast of demand for period 7?
   a. 23.2
   b. 25.3
   c. 27.4
   d. 40
   e. cannot be determined

4. Using a naïve method and four-period seasonality, what is the forecast for period 8?

Period	1	2	3	4	5	6	7	8
Demand	22	25	20	28	21	26		

   a. 26
   b. 21
   c. 28
   d. 24
   e. cannot be determined

A company has the following information on the sales of their product along with other possibly useful information:

Year	Sales ($)	Disposable Income ($)	Mortgage Rate (%)
1991	550	27	8.6
1992	600	29	7.9
1993	605	30	7.3
1994	645	37	7.1
1995	690	45	6.2
1996	750	47	5.5
1997	800	50	5.1
1998	825	51	5.1

5. What could we hypothesize about this product's sales?
   a. There is no relationship between sales and the year.
   b. Disposable personal income is influential in determining the product's sales.
   c. It would add value to graph each variable as they indicate the data are cyclical.
   d. Mortgage rates are not related to sales of this product.
   e. Regression methods are not likely to predict this product's sales.

6. Which planner has done the best job?

	MAPE
Planner A	25%
Planner B	30%
Planner C	35%

  a. Planner A
  b. Planner B
  c. Planner C
  d. Not enough information given

Answers: 1 (a), 2 (b), 3 (25.3 + 2.1*7 = 40), 4 (c), 5 (b), 6 (a)

The Manufacturing Environment

6

I n the case of supply chains that produce goods rather than services, a product will be manufactured somewhere along the supply chain. It may be produced at the firm selling the product or wholly outsourced to another company.

The **manufacturing process** is the series of operations performed to make something. Manufacturing processes can be arranged in one of several layouts: process, product, cellular, or fixed position. Manufacturing processes are categorized based on the strategic use and placement of inventories. These categories include the following:

Make-to-stock. Demand is filled from existing stocks, and production orders are used to replenish those stocks. This is also called **produce-to-stock**.

Package-to-order. A production environment in which a good or service can be packaged after receipt of a customer order. The item is common across many different customers; packaging makes a unique end product.

Assemble-to-order. A production environment where a good or service can be assembled after receipt of a customer's order. This is also called **finish-to-order**.

Mass customization. The creation of a high-volume product with large variety so that a customer may specify an exact model out of a large volume of possible end items while manufacturing cost is low due to the large volume. An example is a personal computer order in which the customer may specify processor speed, memory size, hard disk size and speed, removable storage device characteristics, and many other options when PCs are assembled on one line and at low cost.

Make-to-order. Products are produced after the customer orders arrive. This is also called **produce-to-order**. Where options or accessories are stocked before customer orders arrive, the term **assemble-to-order** is frequently used.

Engineer-to-order. Products whose customer specifications require unique engineering design, significant customization, or new purchased materials. Each customer order results in a unique set of part numbers, along with engineering data such as bills of material and routings. This is also called **design-to-order**.

Lean manufacturing is a philosophy of production that emphasizes the minimization of the amount of all the resources (including time) used in the various activities of the enterprise. It involves identifying and eliminating non-value-added activities in design, production, supply chain management, and interactions with customers. Lean producers employ teams of multiskilled workers at all levels of the organization and use highly flexible, increasingly automated machines to produce large volumes of products in potentially enormous variety. The concept includes a set of principles and practices to reduce cost through the relentless removal of waste and through the simplification of all manufacturing and support processes. A specific emphasis is the minimization of **change-over** (or **setup**) time and cost associated with preparing equipment for production of the next scheduled item. The flexibility to produce in small quantities with little penalty in time and cost is essential to lean manufacturing.

Lean supply chains take the concepts of lean manufacturing and systematically apply them across the chain to identify and eliminate waste (non-value-added activities). Companies recognize that improvements made in one area of the company in isolation do not always result in overall improvements. The same is true across the supply chain. A firm may have made significant strides in eliminating waste by implementing lean concepts at its facility, and further improvements may require working closely to implement lean strategies at a supplier or customer's location. Processes may be completed across companies, and elimination of waste requires working together. Cross-company processes include the following:

planning process capability at each company,

replenishing stock to the end customer,

flowing product along the chain,

paying supply chain partners, and

processing returned goods along the chain.

DECISION MODELS IN SUPPLY CHAINS

To make supply chain decisions, specific alternatives are identified that represent the choices available and criteria for evaluating those alternatives. Decision problems can be formalized by using a **model**.

A **model** is an abstraction or representation of the real system that captures the most important features of a problem and presents them in a form that is easy to interpret. A model can be a written or a verbal description of something. Often a visual representation such as a graph or flow chart is useful.

A **decision model** is the mathematical representation of a problem or business situation developed from theory or observation that is used to understand the relationship between available decision alternatives. Simple decision models can be analyzed with spreadsheets.

There are many different decision models useful for supply chain management, which will be discussed in each section of this book.

We will illustrate the **break-even decision model**, a basic model that is useful in many supply chain situations.

BREAK-EVEN DECISION MODEL

Consider a manufacturer that must decide whether to produce a part in-house or outsource production to a supplier. The manufacturer can produce the part for $130/unit with a fixed (setup) cost of $50,000. The alternative is to outsource the part to a supplier at a cost of $180/unit. At what break-even quantity would the manufacturer want to manufacturer the part in-house?

Solution

The manufacturing cost is expressed in a mathematical equation as

Manufacturing Cost = $50,000 + $130/unit × Quantity Needed

The outsourcing cost is expressed mathematically as

Outsourcing Cost = $180/unit × Quantity Needed

A break-even quantity needed is calculated by setting the equation for manufacturing cost equal to the outsourcing cost equation.

$50,000 + $130/units × Quantity Needed = $180/unit × Quantity Needed

To solve for the break-even quantity needed

$50,000 = ($180/unit − $130/unit) × Quantity Needed

$50,000/($50/unit) = Quantity Needed

1,000 units = Quantity Needed

If the demand is less than 1,000 units, it is more economical to outsource the part. If demand is greater than 1,000 units, it is more economical to manufacture the part in-house.

PRODUCT MIX MODEL

(A spreadsheet titled *Product Mix Problem Templates* that contains this example is available at http://www.oscm-pro.com/scp/.)

Suppose that a manufacturer makes four models of a product and must decide how many units of each product to produce in a given time period to maximize profit. A manufacturer of gas cooking grills produces products A, B, C, and D. Each grill must flow through five departments in the manufacturing plant: stamping, painting, assembly, inspection, and packaging. Relevant data are shown in the following tables:

Grill Model	Selling Price/Unit	Variable Cost/Unit	Minimum Monthly Sales Requirements	Maximum Monthly Sales Potential
A	$250	$210	0	4,000
B	$300	$240	0	3,000
C	$400	$300	500	2,000
D	$650	$520	500	1,000

Here the production rates are given for making each grill model in each department. For example, in the stamping department, grill A is made at a rate of 40 per hour (note: grill A is not painted).

Department	A	B	C	D	Hours Available
Stamping	40	30	10	10	320
Painting	--	20	10	10	320
Assembly	25	15	15	12	320
Inspection	20	20	25	15	320
Packaging	50	40	40	30	320

Given these data, how many units of each grill model should the manufacturing plant make in order to maximize monthly profit?

Solution

This problem can be solved by formulating it as a linear optimization model.

Define:

A, B, C, and D = number of units of models A, B, C, and D to produce.

Maximize Profit = $(250 - 210) \times A + (300 - 240) \times B + (400 - 300) \times C + (650 - 520) \times D$

This is subject to the minimum and maximum sales constraints:

$A \geq 0$ and $A \leq 4,000$

$B \geq 0$ and $A \leq 3,000$

$C \geq 500$ and $C \leq 2,000$

$D \geq 500$ and $D \leq 1,000$

Because the decision variables are defined in units and the capacity constraints are expressed in hours, it is necessary to convert units to the number of hours needed to produce each unit in each department. For example, stamping can produce 40 As per hour, so one unit takes $1/40 = 0.025$ hours to produce. The capacity constraints are

$A/40 + B/30 + C/10 + D/10 \leq 320$	Stamping
$B/20 + C/10 + D/10 \leq 320$	Painting
$A/25 + B/15 + C/15 + D/12 \leq 320$	Assembly

$$A/20 + B/20 + C/25 + D/15 \leq 320 \qquad \text{Inspection}$$

$$A/50 + B/40 + C/40 + D/30 \leq 320 \qquad \text{Packaging}$$

The problem is setup in Excel as follows:

	A	B	C	D	E	F	G
F16			f_x =SUM(B16:E16)				
1	Grill Model	Selling Price/Unit	Variable Cost/Unit	Minimum Monthly Sales Requirements	Maximum Monthly Sales Potential		
2	A	$250	$210	0	4,000		
3	B	$300	$240	0	3,000		
4	C	$400	$300	500	2,000		
5	D	$650	$520	500	1,000		
6							
7	Department	A	B	C	D	Hours Available	
8	Stamping	40	30	10	10	320	
9	Painting	--	20	10	10	320	
10	Assembly	25	15	15	12	320	
11	Inspection	20	20	25	15	320	
12	Packaging	50	40	40	30	320	
13							
14		A	B	C	D	Total	
15	Production	3,857.14	0.00	1,235.71	1,000.00	6,092.86	
16	Profit	$154,285.71	$0.00	$123,571.43	$130,000.00	$407,857.14	
17							
18	Stamping	96.43	0.00	123.57	100.00	320.00	
19	Painting		0.00	123.57	100.00	223.57	
20	Assembly	154.29	0.00	82.38	83.33	320.00	
21	Inspection	192.86	0.00	49.43	66.67	308.95	
22	Packaging	77.14	0.00	30.89	33.33	141.37	

Product Mix

The solver parameters are then defined. Here profit is defined in cell F16. The sales constraints are then defined, followed by the capacity constraints. Because all of the equations are linear, the Simplex LP solving method is used to obtain an optimal solution to the model. The "Simplex LP" method is a mathematical procedure that will find the best solution to this type of problem.

Solver Parameters

Set Objective: $F$16

To: ● Max ○ Min ○ Value Of: 0

By Changing Variable Cells:
$B$15:$E$15

Subject to the Constraints:
$B$15 <= $E$2
$C$15 <= $E$3
$D$15 <= $E$4
$D$15 >= $D$4
$E$15 <= $E$5
$E$15 >= $D$5
$F$18:$F$22 <= $F$8:$F$12

Add
Change
Delete
Reset All
Load/Save

☑ Make Unconstrained Variables Non-Negative

Select a Solving Method: Simplex LP   Options

Solving Method
Select the GRG Nonlinear engine for Solver Problems that are smooth nonlinear. Select the LP Simplex engine for linear Solver Problems, and select the Evolutionary engine for Solver problems that are non-smooth.

Help   Solve   Close

BREAK-EVEN PROBLEMS

(Note: A spreadsheet template for the example and these problems titled *Breakeven Decision Model – Templates* is available at http://www.oscm-pro.com/scp/.)

1) You drive your own car on company business, and your employer reimburses you for such travel at the rate of $0.56 per mile. You estimate that your fixed costs per year such as taxes, insurance, and depreciation are $3,052. The direct or variable costs such as gas, oil, and maintenance average about $0.244 per mile. How many miles must you drive to break even?

2) Suppose that a manufacturer can produce a part for $9 with a fixed cost of $4,000. The manufacturer can contract with a supplier in Asia to purchase the part at a cost of $12, which includes transportation.

   a) If the anticipated production volume is 1,000 units, compute the total cost of manufacturing and total cost of outsourcing. What is the best decision?

   b) Find the break-even volume and characterize the range of volumes for which it is more economical to produce or to outsource. A Data Table can be useful for this analysis (see Appendix A).

3) AudioCables, Inc., is currently manufacturing an adapter that has a variable cost of $0.50 per unit and a selling price of $1.00 per unit. Fixed costs are $14,000. Current sales volume is 30,000 units. The firm can substantially improve the product quality by adding a new piece of equipment at an additional fixed cost of $6,000. Variable costs would increase to $0.60, but sales volume should jump to 50,000 units due to a higher-quality product. Should AudioCables buy the new equipment? Justify your answer using your analysis.

4) Suppose a manufacturer has identified the following options for obtaining a machined part. The manufacturer can

   • buy the part at $200 per unit (including materials), or
   • make the part on a numerically controlled semiautomatic lathe at $75 per unit (including materials) or
   • make the part on a machining center at $15 per unit (including materials).

   There is negligible fixed cost if the item is purchased: a semiautomatic lathe costs $80,000, and a machining center costs $200,000.
   Assume the semiautomatic lathe or the machining center would need to be purchased if these options are chosen and that the full cost of purchasing this equipment is considered in this decision. Also assume that the part sells for $300 each.

   a) What would be the best choice if expected demand were:

   500 units?
   1,000 units?
   2,500 units?

b) What are the break-even points for each option? A Data Table can be useful for this analysis (see Appendix A).

PRODUCT MIX PROBLEM

(Data for this problem is contained in *Product Mix Problem Templates* at http://www.oscm-pro.com/scp/.)

1) Roberto's Honey Farm in Chile makes five types of honey: cream, filtered, pasteurized, mélange (a mixture of several types), and strained, which are sold in 1-kilogram and 0.5-kilogram glass containers, 1-kilogram and 0.75-kilogram plastic containers, or in bulk. The farm can produce a total of 10,000 kilograms of honey. Key data are shown in the following tables.

This table shows the selling prices for the types of honey sold by the farm. Note there are 25 different variations sold because each type of honey is sold in 5 different ways.

Selling Prices (in Chilean Pesos)				
	0.75-kg Plastic	1-kg Plastic	0.5-kg Glass	1-kg Glass	Bulk/kg
Cream	744	880	760	990	616
Filtered	635	744	678	840	521
Pasteurized	696	821	711	930	575
Mélange	669	787	683	890	551
Strained	683	804	697	910	563

The minimum demand that must be met is given in this table. Note there is no minimum for honey that is sold in bulk.

Minimum Demand				
	0.75-kg Plastic	1-kg Plastic	0.5-kg Glass	1-kg Glass
Cream	300	250	350	200
Filtered	250	240	300	180
Pasteurized	230	230	350	300
Mélange	350	300	250	350
Strained	360	350	250	380

This table gives the maximum demand for each product variation. There is no maximum demand for honey sold in bulk since excess product can always be sold in bulk.

Packaging, harvesting and production costs are given in these tables. All product variations must be harvested and produced, but only those product variations that are *not* sold in bulk need to be packaged.

Maximum Demand				
	0.75-kg Plastic	**1-kg Plastic**	**0.5-kg Glass**	**1-kg Glass**
Cream	550	350	470	310
Filtered	400	380	440	300
Pasteurized	360	390	490	400
Mélange	530	410	390	430
Strained	480	420	380	500

Harvesting and Production Costs (in Chilean Pesos) per Kilogram	
Cream	322
Filtered	255
Pasteurized	305
Mélange	272
Strained	287

Package Cost (in Chilean Pesos)			
0.75-kg Plastic	**1-kg Plastic**	**0.5-kg Glass**	**1-kg Glass**
91	112	276	351

a) Develop a linear optimization model to maximize profit if a total of 10,000 kilograms of honey are available. How much of each type of honey should the farm produce to maximize profit?

STUDY QUESTIONS

1. A firm producing medical equipment to customer specification is most likely using a
   a. make-to-stock strategy.
   b. make-to order strategy.
   c. assemble-to-order strategy.
   d. mass production strategy.
   e. Both A and D

2. This is a philosophy of production that emphasizes minimizing cost and time:
   a. changeover management
   b. lean manufacturing
   c. quick production
   d. mass customization

3. Which of the following does not refer to a type of production environment?
   a. make-to-stock
   b. make-to-order
   c. assemble-to-order
   d. fabricate-in-place

Answers: 1 (b), 2 (b), 3 (d)

Supply Chain Strategy and Design

7

PLANNING

Strategic planning is the process of identifying how a company will function in its competitive environment. The **strategic plan** determines actions to support the mission, goals, and objectives of an organization. Generally the plan includes the specific actions needed to achieve those goals and objectives. The strategic plan sets the direction for the organization's marketing strategy and for the resources to allocate to the plan through the supply chain strategy.

Supply chain strategy is made up of the decisions that shape the long-term capabilities of the company's supply chain functions and their contribution to overall strategy through the ongoing reconciliation of market requirements and supply chain resources. Rather than looking at just one company, this strategy addresses the capabilities of all supply chain members, seeking to leverage the resources, skills, strategies, and actions of each one to deliver exceptional value to the end customer.

For example, a company might choose a strategy of customization, or creating products specific to customer needs. Marketing must work with engineering to develop systems to design unique products for each customer. The supply chain must work with manufacturing and suppliers to acquire resources to produce products specific to each order. That contrasts with a strategy of producing a high-volume, low-cost, repetitive product.

The strategic plan is operationalized through intermediate-term tactical plans and short-term operational plans.

The **tactical plans** are functional plans (e.g., for production, sales, marketing) synchronizing activities across functions that specify levels of production, capacity, staffing, funding, and so on, for achieving the intermediate goals and objectives to support the organization's strategic plan.

Operational plans are short-range schedules of specific actions. Operational plans are more detailed than strategic and tactical plans and cover a shorter time horizon.

P&G is a widely known company in the consumer products industry. P&G focuses on five core strengths to set its strategic direction including consumer understanding, innovation, brand building, go-to-market capabilities, and scale. Its strategic plan outlines the future plans for products such as Tide soap based on those five strengths. The supply chain strategy would include decisions on what plants will produce Tide and the required resources, both people and equipment, needed for production. A tactical plan for Tide would include the quantity to produce at each location, as well as the different SKUs that make up the family of Tide. An operational plan for Tide could be the weekly schedule of each variety to be produced on each shift at the plant.

There are three basic supply chain strategies that companies can focus on while recognizing that most companies would be somewhere in the middle across the strategies. The first is a focus on cost minimization. Companies with a cost strategy focus on operating expense management, low-cost inputs and are driven by earnings. A second strategy is a focus on flexibility. Companies with a flexibility strategy focus on supply chain execution and getting the right product to the right place at the right time. They are driven by balance sheet performance, including a careful evaluation of where and how much inventory to have in place. The third strategy focuses on innovation and customization. Companies that use this strategy use the supply chain for rapid, frequent new-product introduction and may build unique products or capabilities for customers. They are driven to accelerate revenue through the addition of new products and customers.

GLOBALIZATION AND PARTNERING

A **global strategy** focuses on improving worldwide performance through the sales and marketing of common goods and services with minimum product variation by country. Its competitive advantage grows through selecting the best locations for operations in other countries. The global strategy is **market driven**, meaning that it is a response to the customers' needs.

In many cases a **multicountry strategy** is needed. This is a strategy in which each country market is self-contained. Customers have unique product expectations that are addressed by local production capabilities.

The global strategy is driven by **business intelligence**, the information collected by an organization on customers, competitors, products or services, and processes. The process of collecting this information is known as **marketing research**, which is the systematic gathering, recording, and analyzing of data relating to the marketing of goods and services. Such research may be undertaken by impartial agencies or by business firms or their agents. Marketing research includes several types: (1) Market analysis (e.g., product potential) is the study of the size, location, nature, and characteristics of markets; (2) sales analysis (or research) is the systematic study and comparison of sales (or consumption) data; (3) consumer research (e.g., motivation research) is concerned with the discovery and analysis of consumer attitudes, reactions, and preferences.

A firm's **market share** is the actual portion of current market demand that a company or product achieves relative to the total demand for the item.

Often companies work together to serve the needs of a market. **Collaborative planning, forecasting**, and **replenishment (CPFR)** is a collaboration process whereby supply chain trading partners can jointly plan key supply chain activities from production and delivery of raw materials to production and delivery of final products to end customers. Collaboration encompasses business planning, sales forecasting, and all operations required to replenish raw materials and finished goods. To facilitate CPFR, access to demand, inventory, and production information is often given to trading partners. This is referred to as **inventory and supply chain visibility**.

There are many types of formal arrangements that are established between cooperating companies. The list below describes several of these relationships.

The **joint venture** is mainly a financial agreement between two or more firms to risk equity capital to attempt a specific business objective. Details of the actual production and distribution of goods are left to the companies in which the firms invest.

A *keiretsu* is a cooperative relationship among companies in Japan where the companies largely remain legally and economically independent, even though they work closely in various ways such as sole sourcing and financial backing. A member of a *keiretsu* generally owns a limited amount of stock in other member companies. A *keiretsu* generally forms around a bank and a trading company, but "distribution" (supply chain) *keiretsu* alliances have been formed of companies ranging from raw material suppliers to retailers.

A **partnership** is a form of business ownership that is not organized as a separate legal entity (i.e., unincorporated business) but entails ownership by two or more persons. In a supply chain context, partnerships are a relationship based on trust, shared risk, and rewards aimed toward achieving a competitive advantage. This is often used with companies that complement each other in some significant way. For example, one company might produce a product and another might distribute and sell the product.

A **strategic alliance** is a more integrated relationship (compared to a partnership) formed by two or more organizations that share information (proprietary), participate in joint investments, and develop linked and common processes to increase the performance of both companies. Many organizations form strategic alliances to increase the performance of their common supply chain.

Companies may form a **virtual organization**, which is a short-term alliance between independent organizations in a potentially long-term relationship. The short-term alliance might be formed to design, produce, and distribute a specific new product. Organizations cooperate based on mutual values and act as a single entity to third parties.

A **horizontal merger** is an alliance between of two or more competing firms. A **vertical merger** is an alliance of two firms where one firm is a supplier to the other.

Joint venture example: Shell Global and ExxonMobil. Infineum International Ltd. is a joint venture of Shell Global and ExxonMobil. The business entity manufacturers and markets fuel lubricants and specialty additives for global customers.

Partnership example: State Farm Insurance and Ford. State Farm and auto manufacturer Ford have united to develop an on-board system to analyze people's driving habits. The insurer plans to use the data to calculate specific insurance rates for each of its customers.

Strategic alliance example: Hewlett Packard and Disney. Hewlett-Packard (HP) and Disney have a long-standing alliance, starting back in 1938, when Disney purchased eight oscillators to use in the sound design of Fantasia from HP founders Bill Hewlett and Dave Packard. When Disney wanted to develop a virtual attraction called Mission: SPACE, Disney Imagineers and HP engineers relied on HP's IT architecture, servers, and workstations to create Disney's most technologically advanced attraction.

Regardless of which type of relationship supply chain companies choose, they require a means of exchanging information. There are several methods in use today to exchange information in electronic format. An **enterprise resources portal** is often associated with an enterprise resources planning system, which can be configured to share or present such information via an Internet portal or hyperlink. An enterprise resources portal can also be one means of implementing a private trading exchange. The following terminologies relate to conducting business over the Internet:

Electronic commerce (e-commerce) is when computer and telecommunication technologies are used to conduct business via electronic transfer of data and documents.

Electronic data interchange (EDI) is the paperless exchange of trading documents, such as purchase orders, shipment authorizations, advanced shipment notices, and invoices, using standardized document formats (electronic documents).

Electronic documents are the digital representation of documents that can be printed.

A **private trading exchange (PTX)** is hosted by a single company to facilitate collaborative e-commerce with its trading partners. As opposed to public e-marketplaces, a private exchange provides the host company with control over many factors, including who may participate (and in what manner), how participants may be connected, and what contents should be presented (and to whom). The ultimate goal might be to improve supply chain efficiencies and responsiveness through improved process visibility and collaboration, advanced integration platforms, and customization capabilities.

Business-to-business commerce (B2B) is business conducted over the Internet between companies. The implication is that this connectivity will cause businesses to transform themselves via supply chain management to become virtual organizations.

Business-to-consumer sales (B2C) is business being conducted between companies and final consumers largely over the Internet. It includes traditional brick-and-mortar businesses that also offer products online and businesses that trade exclusively electronically.

Consortia trade exchanges (CTX) are online marketplaces, usually owned by a third party that allows members to trade with each other.

A **horizontal marketplace** is an online marketplace used by buyers and sellers from multiple industries. This marketplace lowers prices by lowering transaction costs.

Global supply chain companies have special issues to manage related to doing business internationally. **International commercial terms (incoterms)** are created to simplify international transactions by standardizing contract documents. A **tariff** is an official schedule of taxes and fees imposed by a country on imports or exports.

A **trade bloc** or **trading bloc** is a formal agreement between countries intended to reduce or remove barriers to trade within member countries. Frequently, but not always, the countries involved are geographically close. Examples are the following:

The **European Economic Community** was formed by all the major European trade partners including Belgium, Denmark, France, Germany, Greece, Ireland, Italy, Luxembourg, Netherlands, Portugal, Spain, and the United Kingdom. With the formation of the European Union it now includes 16 additional countries.

North American Free Trade Agreement (NAFTA) is an agreement between Canada, Mexico, and the United States that created a rules-based trade bloc in North America. The main impact of the agreement was the elimination of most of the tariffs between Mexico and the United States, and between the United States and Canada. The agreement also has provisions to protect the intellectual property right of products.

Southern Common Market (Mercosur) is a market/customs alliance between Argentina, Brazil, Paraguay, Uruguay, Venezuela, and Bolivia to promote free trade and the easy movement of goods, people, and currency among the countries.

SUPPLY CHAIN DESIGN MODELS

The supply chain strategy defines what resources are needed to support the organization's strategy. Those resources, both in-house and outsourced, may be deployed at facilities around the globe. **Supply chain design** involves the decisions about the structure of the supply chain and the location of processes. These include the locations and capacities of facilities, the products to be made or stored at various locations, modes of transportation, and the information systems needed to link the facilities. Supply chain design decisions support strategic objectives and are often long term and expensive to reverse and must take into account market uncertainty

Designing the supply chain network is critical to successful supply chain management. Many alternatives are often available for how products are sourced through suppliers and manufacturing plants, and distributed using distribution centers, warehouses, and fulfillment centers. Designing an efficient supply chain network relates to minimizing the network related costs, particularly those associated with the movement of items through the network.

Efficient supply chains are designed for low cost by minimizing inventory and maximizing efficiencies in process flow. These supply chains are used for functional products with predictable demand and long life cycles. The goal is to minimize cost while providing reliable and high service levels. An example of an efficient supply chain would be one for a product like canned tomato soup, where a highly repetitive production process is used to produce high volumes of undifferentiated products at the lowest cost.

Responsive supply chains focus on flexibility and responsive service and are able to react quickly to changing market demand and requirements. These supply chains are used for innovative products with unpredictable short-lived demand and high risk of obsolescence. The goal is to minimize inventory and focus on speed and flexibility. These supply chains are by nature more risky and risk and return are linked—the highest profit margin with the highest risk of uncertainty in demand. Companies seek to reduce uncertainty, cut lead times, add flexibility, or hedge against uncertainty with inventory buffers and excess capacity. A responsive supply chain would be used for producing cell phones where demand is difficult to predict and new models are introduced frequently.

With companies producing a wide range of products today, supply chains may be segmented to best match products to supply chains. **Supply chain segmentation** is the creation of quite different supply chains that may function alongside each other to match products to market requirements.

The design of the network is part of the strategic planning process because how items flow is a repetitive process that is executed virtually every day that the firm operates. A well-designed network relative to costs incurred and responsiveness can give the firm a significant competitive advantage, whereas a poor network can be an ongoing burden to the firm.

A supply chain map may be used to display the dynamics that govern how a supply chain works and create a physical picture of the supply chain. Think of it as flying in an airplane at 30,000 feet and looking down to follow the movement of a particular product. The map can be used to evaluate the effectiveness of the link between supply chain strategy and corporate strategy. For instance, a strategy of selling a low-cost product may require production in low-cost locations. The map provides a clear picture of a material's origin, movement, and destination, and can alert the company to possible constraints. It provides a communication tool to be used across functions and with suppliers and customers to provide a common understanding of the supply chain. The map can be used to challenge current methods and identify opportunities to improve, thereby supporting network redesign. Many consumers today are concerned about the origin of products they purchase and the working conditions at companies producing those products. They may choose products based on the environmental impact of the product. Mapping the product's components will help them understand their choices.

LOCATING FACILITIES

A useful model for analyzing supply chain networks is commonly referred to as the **plant location model**. This basic model can be used in many different ways, including analysis of problems related to getting supply to manufacturing plant, locating manufacturing plants, and getting products from manufacturing plant to warehouse/distribution centers.

To illustrate how the plant location model can be used to analyze the attractiveness of a supply chain network design, consider the following example problem.

EXAMPLE: PLANT LOCATION MODEL

(Note: A spreadsheet with this example titled *Plant Location Problem Templates* is available at http://www.oscm-pro.com/scp/.)

A firm is deciding where to source a new product that will be sold in the United States, Europe, and China. The firm is considering options for sourcing the product at either a manufacturing plant located in Nogales, Mexico or Taiwan, People's Republic of China; or a combination of the two.

The firm expects demand during the first year to be the following: United States: 10,000 units; Europe: 5,000 units; China: 7,000 units.

The cost to produce the product is the same whether it is produced in the Nogales or the Taiwan plant. Each individual plant can produce the total expected demand or some portion of the total demand. The product can be shipped from Nogales or Taiwan to the firm's markets according to the following schedule of shipping cost per unit:

	United States	Europe	China
Nogales	$100/unit	$200/unit	$250/unit
Taiwan	$225/unit	$175/unit	$75/unit

Should the firm source only from either Nogales or Taiwan, or from a combination of Nogales and Taiwan?

Solution

The cost to source from Nogales to the three markets is

Cost of Nogales to United States = $100/unit × 10,000 units = $1,000,000

Cost of Nogales to Europe = $200/unit × 5,000 units = $1,000,000

Cost of Nogales to China = $250/unit × 7,000 units = $1,750,000

Total of using only Nogales = $3,750,000

The cost to source from Taiwan to the three markets is

Cost of Taiwan to United States = $225/unit × 10,000 units = $2,250,000

Cost of Taiwan to Europe = $175/unit × 5,000 units = $875,000

Cost of Taiwan to China = $75/unit × 7,000 units = $525,000

Total cost of using only Taiwan = $3,650,000

The best single-source option is Taiwan.

To evaluate using a combination of Nogales and Taiwan, the cost matrix can be analyzed to find the least-cost plant to serve each market. In the case of the United States,

Nogales would be used at a cost of $1,000,000 = $100/unit × 10,000 units. For Europe, Taiwan would be used costing $875,000 = $175/unit × 5,000 units. Finally, China would be served by Taiwan for $525,000 = $75/unit × 7,000 units. The total cost for this combination is: $2,400,000.

Using a combination of plants would be best relative to cost.

There can be many variations on the problem including the imposition of capacity limits on the plants. Different cost structures can also be considered, including the fixed cost associated with using a plant, for example. More complex problems can be analyzed using the Solver option in Excel. Examples of these extensions to the problem are in *Plant Location Problem Templates* available from http://www.oscm-pro.com/scp.

VEHICLE ROUTING

Another important problem that relates to efficiently serving a supply chain involves the routing of vehicles for the purpose of delivering goods to customers. There are many variations on the problem, but one example is the home delivery of prescription orders by a pharmacy. Here the problem is finding the shortest route for delivering to each customer site, in essence creating a loop from the warehouse or fulfillment center, visiting each customer location and then returning to the warehouse. The goal is to minimize the total distance traveled over the loop. Mathematicians often refer to this as the **traveling salesman problem**, harking back to the days when salesmen traveled from customer to customer on regular routes, soliciting orders from businesses such as doctors' offices, retail stores, pharmacies, hardware stores, people's homes, etc.

EXAMPLE: VEHICLE ROUTING PROBLEM

(Note: This example problem is included in the spreadsheet titled *Vehicle Routing Problems* and is available at http://www.oscm-pro.com/scp/.)

Consider the problem that a company has for delivering product to dealers in the Midwest region of the United States. The dealers are located in Minneapolis, Milwaukee, Des Moines, Chicago, Detroit, St. Louis, Kansas City, Indianapolis, Cleveland, and Cincinnati. The company sends a single truck on a weekly run through these cities, starting from and returning to its plant in Milwaukee. The goal is to find the shortest loop that connects these cities.

The following table has highway travel distances in miles between these cities:

From/To	Minneapolis	Milwaukee	Des Moines	Chicago	Detroit	St. Louis	Kansas City	Indianapolis	Cleveland	Cincinnati
Minneapolis	0	337	244	410	690	561	437	592	752	707
Milwaukee	337	0	374	90	370	382	567	280	433	395
Des Moines	244	374	0	334	599	349	194	473	662	589
Chicago	410	90	334	0	281	295	509	180	343	295
Detroit	690	370	599	281	0	531	765	282	170	258
St. Louis	561	382	349	295	531	0	248	243	561	351
Kansas City	437	567	194	509	765	248	0	483	801	591
Indianapolis	592	280	473	180	282	243	483	0	317	114
Cleveland	752	433	662	343	170	561	801	317	0	244
Cincinnati	707	395	589	295	258	351	591	114	244	0

Solution

Finding a solution to this problem uses a feature of the Excel Solver that restricts the solution values to be integers that each have a different value. This constraint type is called "AllDifferent."

To solve the problem, first setup a table with the distances as shown. The solution will be generated by Solver in the "Order" columns B15 through B24. We use the VLOOKUP function to find the name of the city in the "City" column. For example, the function in A15 is LOOKUP(B15,$A$2:$B$11,2) which finds the city number in B15 in column A in the range of cells $A$2:$B$11 and returns the name of the city from column 2 of that table. The distances are found from the table using the INDEX function. The function in C15 is INDEX($C$2:$L$11,B15,B24), which finds the distance between the city indexed in B15 and B24 (Cleveland and Cincinnati). This first distance cell is defined to force the loop between the cities. Cells C16 through C24 link the current row to the previous. For example, cell C16 is INDEX($C$2:$L$11, B16,B15).

		Minneapolis	Milwaukee	Des Moines	Chicago	Detroit	St. Louis	Kansas City	Indianapolis	Cleveland	Cincinnati
1	Minneapolis	0	337	244	410	690	561	437	592	752	707
2	Milwaukee	337	0	374	90	370	382	567	280	433	395
3	Des Moines	244	374	0	334	599	349	194	473	662	589
4	Chicago	410	90	334	0	281	295	509	180	343	295
5	Detroit	690	370	599	281	0	531	765	282	170	258
6	St. Louis	561	382	349	295	531	0	248	243	561	351
7	Kansas City	437	567	194	509	765	248	0	483	801	591
8	Indianapolis	592	280	473	180	282	243	483	0	317	114
9	Cleveland	752	433	662	343	170	561	801	317	0	244
10	Cincinnati	707	395	589	295	258	351	591	114	244	0

City	Order	Distance
Chicago	4	90
Detroit	5	281
Cleveland	9	170
Cincinnati	10	244
Indianapolis	8	114
St. Louis	6	243
Kansas City	7	248
Des Moines	3	194
Minneapolis	1	244
Milwaukee	2	337
	Total Miles	2,165

The Solver is then setup to minimize Total Miles, which is the sum of the distances, by changing the order of the cities indexed in B15:B24. The AllDifferent constraint forces each city index to be a different integer number. The best solving method for this problem is the evolutionary solving method. The solution shown is a result from using this method.

The technique will not guarantee an optimal solution to the problem, but it does work fairly well. Trying different starting solutions can often result in different results, so a little experimentation is useful.

LOCATION PROBLEMS

(Note: A template for these problems is contained in *Location Problem Templates* available at http://www.oscm-pro.com/scp/.)

1) Liquid Gold, Inc., transports radioactive waste from nuclear power plants to disposal sites around the country. Each plant has a certain amount of material that must be moved each period. Each disposal site has a limited capacity per period. The cost of transporting between sites is given in the following table (some combinations of plants and storage sites are not to be used, and no figure is given). Develop and solve a location model for this problem.

Plant	Radioactive Waste Material (kilograms)	Cost to Ship to Disposal Site ($/kilogram)				Site	Capacity of Site (kilograms)
		S1	S2	S3	S4		
P1	20,876	$105	$86	--	$23	S1	285,922
P2	50,870	$86	$58	$41	--	S2	308,578
P3	38,652	$93	$46	$65	$38	S3	111,955
P4	28,951	$116	$27	$94	--	S4	208,555
P5	87,423	$88	$56	$82	$89		
P6	76,190	$111	$36	$72	--		
P7	58,237	$169	$65	$48	--		

2) Yummy restaurants use one company, Arctic Freeze, Inc. (AFI), as the source for all products served at their restaurants. AFI negotiates the purchase of the products and coordinates the delivery of cases to each restaurant. Yummy's business is growing with same-store sales expected to grow by 7.5% in 2015 and another 2% in 2016.

Products are shipped from AFI's distribution centers (DCs) to each of the restaurants across the area. The restaurants place orders to the DCs to be replenished on a daily basis. The DCs charge $0.028 per cubic meter (CBM) per mile to move product from the DCs to the restaurants. On average, six cases equate to one cubic meter of volume.

The Phoenix, Fresno, and Santa Fe DCs can no longer handle the volume of product required by the growth of restaurants in the southwest part of the country. AFI and Yummy are considering adding a DC in another southwest location. They have investigated several potential sites and have determined that the best location would be either St. George, UT, or Albuquerque, NM. The cost to build in St. George is estimated to be $3 million, while Albuquerque is expected to cost $2.5 million.

Projected demand in cases for the key cities within the region to be served by the new DC are listed in the following table. After adding a new facility, the existing facilities in Phoenix, Fresno, and Santa Fe will each continue to provide up to 180,000 cases of products to the region.

Stores	Projected Demand in Cases	Distances				
		Miles From Phoenix	Miles from Fresno	Miles from Santa Fe	Miles from St. George	Miles from Albuquerque
Durango, CO	180,000	455	900	210	415	215
Flagstaff, AZ	105,000	145	590	380	270	325
Tucson, AZ	140,000	115	705	510	540	450
Henderson, NV	210,000	280	390	615	135	560
Elko, NV	75,000	730	590	850	405	825
Sacramento, CA	150,000	760	170	1,140	680	1,080
Caliente, CA	80,000	460	140	840	380	785
Farmington, NM	60,000	390	885	210	380	180
Total	1,000,000					

a) Based on the projected demand for cases of product in the key cities in the region, what is the minimum capacity required for the new AFI DC?

b) Using the projected demand, calculate the cost of shipping to the key cities in the region if a DC is built in St. George that can ship 800,000 cases. Recalculate the costs if the DC is built in Albuquerque with the same capacity.

c) What is the total cost of each location? Which city would you select for the new DC?

d) What other issues should AFI consider in making their new DC decision?

VEHICLE ROUTING PROBLEM

(Note: A template for this problem is included in the spreadsheet titled *Vehicle Routing Problems* and is available at http://www.oscm-pro.com/scp/.)

1) Consider a company that needs to deliver and pick up material by van to four sites in a city on a daily basis. The four sites are where customers are located, and these deliveries will be made for the next few weeks. The van will start and return to Barbille, the location of the company, each time that it runs the route. The following table has the distances in kilometers between each site and Barbille.

	Barbille	Castleview	Endford	Downmill	Armbridge
Barbille		5	7	12	8
Castleview	5		7	10	9
Endford	7	7		9	11
Downmill	12	10	9		6
Armbridge	8	9	11	6	

a) Set this problem up as a vehicle routing problem and solve it using the Solver in Excel. What is the shortest route for the truck to follow?

CASE STUDY

IKEA

IKEA Swedish furniture maker IKEA is the world's largest retail furniture chain, with over 300 stores located around the globe. IKEA is known for its low prices and innovative designs, which often include assembling the furniture at the customer's home. Read about IKEA's strategy online (http://www.ikea.com).

a. Describe what customers value when they shop at IKEA. How does the shopping experience at IKEA differ from other retail furniture stores?

b. What are the key components of the supply chain strategy that are necessary to support the company's strategy?

c. IKEA has been expanding globally to China, India, and other parts of the world. Describe some of the challenges of expanding into specific countries for both IKEA and its supply chain.

CASE STUDY

Supply Chain Mapping
LISTERINE

May 28 Our journey begins in Australia where a farmer is harvesting his spring crop of eucalyptus for eucalyptol, the oil found in its leathery leaves. The farmer sells the crop to an Australian processing company, which spends about four weeks extracting the eucalyptol from the eucalyptus. Morris Plains, NJ-based Warner-Lambert (WL) partners with a distributor in New Jersey to buy the oil from the Australian company and transport it to WL's Listerine manufacturing and distribution facility in Lititz, Pa. The load will arrive at Lititz about three months after the harvest, says Robert LeRoy, director of material procurement for WL.

July 13 Half a world away, an operation owned by the Saudi Arabian government is drilling deep under the desert for the natural gas that will yield the synthetic alcohol that gives Listerine its 43-proof punch. Union Carbide Corp. ships the gas via tanker to a refinery in Texas City, TX, which purifies it and converts it into ethanol. The ethanol is loaded onto another tanker and transported from Texas City through the Gulf of Mexico to New Jersey, where it's transferred to storage tanks and transported via truck or rail to WL's plant. A single shipment of ethanol takes about six to eight weeks to get from Saudi Arabia to Lititz.

August 25 SPI Polyols, Inc., a manufacturer of ingredients for the confectionery, pharmaceutical, and oral-care industries, buys corn syrup from one of several corn wet millers that purchases corn from farmers in the Midwest. SPI converts the corn syrup into sorbitol solution, which sweetens and adds bulk to the Cool Mint Listerine. The syrup is shipped to SPI's New Castle, DE, facility for processing and then delivered on a tank wagon to Lititz. The whole process, from the time the corn is harvested to when it's converted into sorbitol, takes about a month.

August 31 By now the solutions of ethanol, eucalyptol, and sorbitol have all arrived at WL's plant in Lititz, where employees test them—along with the menthol, citric acid, and other ingredients that make up Listerine—for quality assurance before authorizing storage in tanks. To mix the ingredients, flow meters turn on valves at each tank and measure out the right proportion, according to the Cool Mint formula developed by WL research and development in 1990. (The original amber mouthwash was developed in 1879.) This blending process is constant; as ingredients are added to the several-thousand gallon vat, the properly blended liquid is continuously transferred to a separate holding tank. Next the Listerine flows through a pipe to fillers along the packaging line. The fillers dispense the product into bottles delivered continuously from a nearby plastics company for just-in-time manufacturing.

The bottles are capped, labeled, and fitted with tamper-resistant safety bands, and then placed in corrugated shipping boxes known as shippers that each hold a dozen 500-milliliter bottles. During this process, machines automatically check for skewed labels, missing safety bands and other problems. The entire production cycle, from the delivery via pipe of the Listerine liquid to the point where bottles are boxed and ready to go, takes a matter of minutes. The line can produce about 300 bottles per minute—a far cry from the 80 to 100 bottles that the line produced per minute prior to 1994. In that year, WL switched from glass bottles to sturdy plastic bottles, modernized its production line with high-speed equipment, and went from mixing batches of mouthwash one tank at a time to the continuous mixing process.

Each shipper travels on a conveyor belt to the palletizer, which organizes and shrink-wraps shippers into 100-case pallets. Stickers with identifying bar codes are affixed to the pallets. Drivers forklift the pallets to the distribution center located in the same Lititz facility and store them in a designated spot where they will sit for two to four weeks.

September 14 WL receives an EDI order from CVS for 20 pallets of 500-milliliter bottles of Cool Mint Listerine to be delivered by September 16 to CVS's Woonsocket, RI warehouse, which serves all New England CVS stores. The order is automatically screened to make sure the numbers requested are reasonable and that the source for the order is legitimate before it is passed on to WL's SAP system, an enterprise resource planning tool from SAP AG. SAP prices the order and determines how much of it is already in stock and how much needs to be manufactured. Generally the order is in stock because the SAP Merchandise Transaction System would've predicted store demand.

That same day, SAP transfers the order to WL's Strategic Transportation Planner made by Manugistics. The Manugistics system determines how best to consolidate order delivery and which shipping companies to use to minimize costs and meet the required delivery time specified by CVS. An action plan specifying those details is drawn up. WL then sends an electronic alert to the chosen shipping companies via EDI.

Meanwhile, the Manugistics action plan is automatically downloaded to SAP, which sends it back to WL's McHugh Software International, Inc., warehouse system around 1 a.m. for use by the people on the WL warehouse floor. The McHugh system specifies how the warehouse employees should pick and ship the day's orders.

September 15 Because CVS usually orders products in volume, the pick quantities tend to be full pallets, so forklifts are used to transport the order instead of WL's network of automatic conveyor belts used for smaller orders. Every morning, the WL forklift operators use computers attached to their forklifts as well as handheld scanners with instruction screens linked to the McHugh system to learn what they need to pick up, where it's located, and where to transport it. When the lift operators get to the appropriate pallet, they scan the bar code with the handheld device so that the software can confirm it's the correct product. They next bring the pallet to the designated shipping door and use the onboard computer system and handheld to inform the McHugh system that the job is finished. Workers at the shipping door then load waiting trucks with the Listerine, Sudafed, Rolaids, Certs, Lubriderm, Schick razors, Neosporin, Bubblicious and other WL products ordered by CVS.

QUESTIONS

a. Draw a high-level map of the Listerine supply chain. Use boxes for each node of the supply chain. Connect the boxes with arrows representing transportation. Draw arrows for information flow. Include lead time on each arrow and box.

b. Identify opportunities for improvement in the supply chain. How would your map change after the improvements?

c. Identify points in the supply chain that are vulnerable to disruption. How could you lessen the impact of each risk?

Managing Customer and Supplier Relationships

8

Today's focus on supply chains makes a case for more thoughtful evaluation of how to manage relationships with both suppliers and customers. The success for a firm may rely on how capable a supplier is in developing and delivering a product to the firm's customer. At the same time, understanding what customers value and how to deliver on that value requires a much closer relationship with the firm's customers. The relationship may extend beyond the first-tier customers to second-tier (the customers' customer) and possibly to the end customer. Supply-side relationships may also go beyond first-tier suppliers to the suppliers' suppliers. Information technology allows for instant sharing of data to all supply chain partners.

A core principle of supply chain management is that all relationships are not equal. For a supplier who provides a product one time on a "spot buy," an arm's-length agreement, where the two parties act independently and have no formal relationship to each other, or an online auction may be appropriate. The supplier who provides a strategic component that is critical to the success of the firm may require a long-term commitment. Regardless of where the company is positioned in the supply chain, its focus must be on customer requirements. For instance, if end customers require a variety of products with short lead times and variable volumes, each partner in the chain must be able to react quickly to ramp production up or down.

SUPPLIER RELATIONSHIPS

Supplier relationship management (SRM) is a comprehensive approach to managing an enterprise's interactions with the organizations that supply the goods and services the enterprise uses. The goal of SRM is to streamline and make more effective the processes between an enterprise and its suppliers. SRM is often associated with automating procure-to-pay business processes, evaluating supplier performance, and exchanging information with suppliers. An e-procurement system often comes under the umbrella of a supplier relationship management family of applications. The terms *vendor* and *supplier* refer to any seller of an item in the marketplace.

The **procurement** functions in a business relate to the planning, purchasing, inventory control, traffic, receiving, incoming inspection, and salvage operations associated with items that are bought by the business. **Purchasing** is the term used for the function responsible for procuring materials, supplies, and services. An important element of purchasing is **sourcing**, which is the process of identifying a company that provides a needed good or service. **Spend management** is managing the flow of funds used to purchase goods and services in a supply chain and includes outsourcing and procurement activities.

An **agent** is a business entity that is authorized to purchases goods and services for another company. The agent is responsible for procuring an item at the lowest cost while ensuring quality, delivery, and other criteria imposed by the buyer. Typically a **sales agent** charges a fee for transactions but does not take the title for the goods. In the case of an international purchase, the sales agent is referred to as an **import broker**. A **purchasing agent** buys and actually takes the title for the goods and services and then resells them to the company.

The **supplier-input-process-output-customer (SIPOC) diagram** is a high-level process map that shows the structure of a firm's procurement functions together with the processes of external suppliers, input processes within the firm, outputs of the firm's transformation processes, and customer linkages. An SIPOC diagram identifies the critical aspects of this integrated process in a simple matter while capturing the critical elements of the system. This is a useful tool for process improvement activities.

Strategic sourcing refers to a comprehensive approach for locating and sourcing key material suppliers, which often includes the business process of analyzing total amount spent for material according to procurement-related cost categories. There is a focus on the development of long-term relationships with trading partners who can help the purchaser meet profitability and customer satisfaction goals. From the perspective of information technology applications, strategic sourcing includes automation of request for quote (RFQ), request for proposal (RFP), electronic auctioning, and contract management processes. A **reverse auction** is one in which suppliers attempt to underbid their competitors for a customer's order. The reverse auction is typically done on the Internet, where company identities are known only by the buyer.

The purchasing process that is focused simply on ordering nonstrategic material is referred to as **tactical buying**. Characteristics for items that can be bought "tactically" include ready and stable availability, standard specifications, predictable delivery, items that are noncritical to production, and high quality material with very little concern for rejects.

A **single-source supplier** is a company that is selected to have 100% of the business although alternate suppliers are available. When there is only one supplier capable of meeting requirements (usually technical) for an item that entity is referred to as a **sole-source supplier**.

Multisourcing is when a good or service is procured from more than one independent supplier.

When there is a long-term commitment to a supplier, often a **blanket purchase order** is issued. This streamlines the process of ordering items from the supplier by eliminating steps that would normally be done with a new supplier.

The **landed cost** of an item includes the product cost plus the costs of logistics, such as warehousing, transportation, and handling fees.

Line-haul costs as defined within physical distribution (actual movement of goods) are cost elements that vary by distance traveled and not by weight carried (e.g., fuel, drivers' wages, wear and tear on the vehicle). When line-haul costs are a major element of the landed cost, the proximity of the supplier to the customer is important.

Supplier certification refers to procedures that verify that a supplier operates in a manner that meets the customer's requirements. Such requirements can include cost, quality, delivery, flexibility, maintenance, safety, and ISO quality and environmental standards. The following supplier scorecard includes some of these requirements.

Supplier Scorecard

Summary

Suppllier Scorecard	Weight	Score	Weighted Score
Quality	50%	5	2.5
Delivery	30%	5	1.5
Customer Satisfaction	10%	4	0.4
Impact Score	10%	5	0.5
Weighted Score =			4.9

Goals	
Quality:	< 650 PPM
Delivery:	> 95%
Customer Satisfaction	5
Quality/Delivery Impact Out of 5 Maximum	5

CUSTOMER RELATIONSHIPS

Customer relationship management (CRM) is a marketing philosophy based on putting the customer first. The concept encompasses the collection and analysis of information needed for sales and marketing decision support, and extends beyond the information needed for simple accounting system support. The goal is to understand and support existing and potential customer needs. It includes such items as account management, catalog and order entry, payment processing, credits and adjustments, and other functions.

The work of CRM is often done by a **manufacturer's representative** or **manufacturer's agent**, a person who sells goods for several firms but does not take title for them. In addition a **distributor** or **wholesaler** may be a part of the supply chain; distributors and wholesalers are businesses that do not manufacture their own products, but rather purchase them from manufacturers and resell them to the final customer. Such a business usually maintains a finished-goods inventory, which makes the process of serving many smaller customers quicker and more efficient. The manufacturing representatives and distributors provide focused services that augment the production or distribution functions inside the organization; examples include handling customer service inquiries and field service, such as training and warranty management.

Common measures of success in CRM are the **customer service ratio** and the **fill rate**. There are many variations, but these measures of delivery performance of finished goods are usually expressed as a percentage, such as the percent of items on an order that are delivered on time and in the proper quantity. Other typical measures are delivery **lead time**, which is the time from when an order is received until it is delivered to the customer. A **quick response program (QRP)** is a system of linking final retail sales with production and shipping schedules back through the chain of supply, which employs point-of-sale scanning and electronic data interchange, and may use direct shipment from a factory to a retailer. Another common approach is a **rapid replenishment** or **continuous replenishment** strategy in which the supplier prepares shipments at predetermined intervals and varies the quantity based on recent sales data. Sales data may be supplied via a point-of-sale system. These strategies are designed to provide the customer with better service while lowering transaction costs for the customer.

Supply chain companies recognize the importance of providing good service to customers but that not all customers are equal nor do they deserve the same high level of service (customer service isn't free). Companies can provide a variety of services to the customer—anything from making personal sales calls to holding dedicated inventory.

One way of identifying the cost to serve a specific customer is to look at **customer profitability**, which can be defined as the revenues from a particular customer minus the costs attributable to that customer.

Customer Profitability = Revenues − Attributable Costs (cost of sales, commission, sales call expense, discounts, order processing costs, promotional costs, merchandising costs, nonstandard packaging, dedicated inventory holding costs and warehouse space, material handling cost, transport cost, documentation/ communication, returns)

The key question to consider is, "What costs would I avoid and what revenues would I lose if I lost this customer?"

The following figure illustrates what the company should do after evaluating service costs. Those customers that are costly to serve (require in-person contacts, dedicated inventory, special handling, etc.) but have high revenue should be cost engineered to determine how to eliminate some of the costs. On the other hand, customers who have a low cost to serve (order online and buy standard products with standard packaging) and have high revenue should be protected as much as possible.

The Cost to Serve a Customer

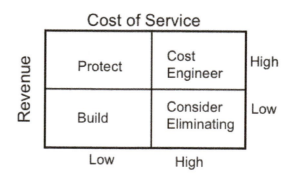

A similar concept states that all customers are not equally profitable. The **Pareto Law**, or 80/20, rule states that 80% of profits come from 20% of customers. That 20%, or A customers, are highly valued and should receive the highest level of service; B customers should be managed carefully; and C customers should be managed fairly and efficiently. The following figure illustrates the application of the Pareto-Law idea to customer profitability.

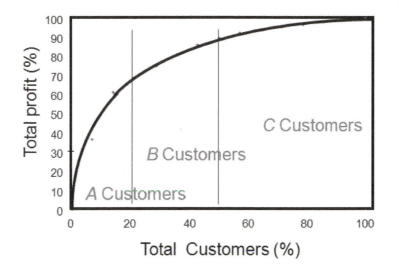

Pareto Assessment of Customer Profitability

In addition to customer profitability, supply chain companies are also interested in the lifetime value of a customer. With unlimited choice available to customers today on where to purchase products, companies are focused on how to get return business from customers. The prime customer service objective may be customer retention. This is evidenced with the growth of loyalty programs.

Lifetime value can be defined as the average transaction value × yearly frequency of purchase × customer's "life expectancy" (length of time the customer is expected to purchase this product). The term *share of wallet* is also used to describe the same concept.

For example, a family of four spends $200 per week on groceries. A local grocery store would like 100% of their business. Over 52 weeks, the customer is worth $10,400 to the store, and if the family lives in the community for 15 years, they are worth $156,000 to the store.

Another popular strategy is referred to as **vendor-managed inventory (VMI)**. With this supply chain concept, performance is optimized by giving the supplier (vendor) access to the customer's inventory data and making the supplier responsible for maintaining the inventory level required by the customer. This activity is accomplished by a process in which resupply is done by the supplier through regularly scheduled reviews of the on-site inventory. The on-site inventory is counted, damaged or outdated goods are removed, and the inventory is restocked to predefined levels. The supplier obtains a receipt for the restocked inventory and accordingly invoices the customer. This is similar to the continuous replenishment strategy described earlier.

In some cases manufacturers and retailers individually experience high variability in demand for their products. A method called **risk pooling** for managing this involves pooling demand for their products and serving this demand through a common inventory. This method is often associated with the **management of inventory risk**. Manufacturers and retailers that experience high variability in demand for their products can pool together common and possibly costly inventory components associated with a broad family of products, e.g., to buffer the overall burden of having to deploy inventory for each individual product. The innovative use of risk pooling strategies can greatly reduce the cost of inventory investment in expensive replacement parts where demand is sporadic and where the cost of a stockout (which is not having the part when needed) is very high.

Hospitals today practice risk pooling by keeping most of the stock of a particular medicine or supply item in a centralized warehouse location at the hospital. Small quantities of each item may be kept at a nursing station in each department and replenished as needed using replenishment orders. The overall amount of inventory at the hospital is reduced by centralizing inventory, and the **safety stock** needed to avoid stockouts is significantly reduced.

REVENUE MANAGEMENT

Most businesses face significant variation in customer demand during the year due to the varying need for the product at different times of the year, competitor pricing strategies, and other factors. **Revenue management** is the use of data-driven strategies that are oriented toward maximizing profit through pricing strategies that alter customer demand patterns. Examples include the discounting of airline flights due to having too much capacity over a route and the use of customer incentive promotions by auto manufacturers.

This strategy typically involves defining a pricing strategy with the objective of creating increased value to a specific customer segment over a period of time. By lowering prices on products, a company can increase demand over weak demand periods and gain market share, which increases revenue as long as the price is more than the marginal cost of the product.

In other cases, where demand is sufficient to fill capacity but there are typically late cancellations (e.g., hotel rooms or airline seats), the firm may overbook to ensure that revenue is maximized by operating at full capacity. Some tactics might involve creating automatic pricing tools that dynamically change price as a direct function of current demand and the real time availability of the resource. This approach is particularly attractive when the resource is perishable, such that after a specific time it is worthless (e.g., a room in a hotel room on a specific date).

The synergy between supply chain management and revenue management is great. Many supply chain processes have significant fixed costs, whether they operate or not. Any activity that maximizes the profitable use of the process is attractive. Revenue management generally assumes that costs and capacity are, to a great extent, fixed, and so prices are set that maximize revenue given these constraints.

RISK IN CUSTOMER AND SUPPLIER RELATIONSHIPS

Despite best efforts to select great suppliers and manage customer relationships, the inherent nature of supply chains makes them risky. Suppliers may experience quality problems, transportation suppliers may have problems clearing customs, and customers may experience financial difficulties making them cancel their orders. These are only just a small sample of the kind of risk in a supply chain. Natural disasters, political strife, and companies' own supply chain practices can add risk. Where most of a product was once built in-house, e.g., the Ford cars produced early in the 19th century, today companies may outsource much of all of their components and products. This, combined with lean practices that reduce inventory along with global sources of supply, makes supply chains much more vulnerable to disruptions.

A **supply chain disruption** is any unplanned and unanticipated event that disrupts the normal flow of goods and materials within the supply chain. Many supply chain practitioners have the perspective that all supply chains are inherently risky: sooner or later a disruption will occur. These same managers consistently list managing supply chain risk as one of their top challenges. Companies have begun creating **risk profiles** to identify potential risks and determine the likelihood of their occurrence. Efforts can then be made to mitigate the risk by lessening the likelihood of it occurring or reducing its impact.

A risk management plan includes the following:

1. Identifying the sources of disruption risks and vulnerabilities
2. Classifying, measuring, and monitoring risk, i.e., mapping the risk and the severity
3. Establishing a risk mitigation plan with goals, metrics, accountability, and triggers that set actions in place

Identifying sources of risk begins with overall knowledge of the supply chain. Supply chain maps can help identify vulnerable points in the chain. Product flows, lead times, inventories, and facility locations must all be identified. Visibility across the supply chain is required. Examples abound of companies caught off guard by problems with a supplier's supplier. External issues such as political situations, weather, and labor issues must be examined. The duration of the event should be noted along with the likely duration of impact.

Risks from natural disasters and weather incidents are easy to identify. However, there are a number of different kinds of risk that are not as obvious. One of the most troubling risks to supply chain managers is demand volatility. Being able to quickly detect changes in demand and then react to them is a necessary part of risk management

Once the risks have been identified, the likelihood and severity of the impact on the company should be estimated. The following risk profile shows how a number of risks might be classified. For risks categorized as 9 (high probability of occurring but low impact), companies often have processes in place. For example, for suppliers who often provide 3 bad parts out of a batch of 100, the company has a plan to sort and return the bad parts with little impact on the company. Risks categorized as 1 (low probability of occurring but a severe impact, such as tornadoes or fires) can often be mitigated by purchasing insurance. The most troubling are those risks with a high likelihood of occurring and severe implications. Systems must be put in place to monitor those events and plans established to mitigate their impact.

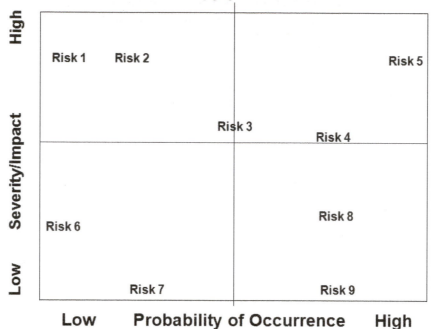

Risk mitigation plans includes steps the company can take to reduce the likelihood of an event happening or to lessen its impact. Specific solutions are required for each risk. For example if a supplier is located in an area with a potential for earthquakes, an alternate supplier in another region or country can be identified. Some companies seek to minimize risk through advance purchases and safety stock. Others seek to mitigate risk severity through contingency planning.

To evaluate their readiness to combat supply chain risk, companies will often use **stress testing**, including group exercises using "what if" scenarios, a technique often used in disaster preparation. Supply chain leaders are given a potential risky situation and evaluate their preparedness and contingency plans. The exercises seek to change the risk exposure of the company and work to improve the continuity of supply in case of a disruption.

STUDY QUESTIONS

1. When companies try to synchronize demand and supply, demand sometimes exceeds supply in a given time period. Companies may try to satisfy demand through building enough capacity to meet peak demand, or they may try to shift demand through
   a. increasing cycle time.
   b. peak period price changes.
   c. reducing resources in peak periods.
   d. better forecasting.

2. By applying the Pareto principle, customers can be segmented by percent of sales into A, B, and C categories. Which of the following statements best characterizes the relationship the firm should have with the A segment?
   a. Members of this group often become tomorrow's "customers of choice."
   b. The business operation provides good levels of standardized customer service to this segment.
   c. Dedicated customer account teams establish a consistent point of contact and a personal touch.
   d. Infrequent communication occurs between the company and these firms because the relationship has been well-defined through contract negotiations.

3. The profitability of a specific customer
   a. asks the key question, "What costs would increase and what revenues would I gain if I lost this customer?"
   b. is evaluated by looking at the total cost of ownership of acquiring that customer.
   c. is evaluated by net sales minus the total cost of serving that customer.
   d. does not include costs such as promotional costs, nonstandard packaging, and dedicated warehouse space for the customer's inventory.

4. In _____ , suppliers bid for a buyer's business.
   a. auctions
   b. collaborative relationships
   c. purchasing strategies
   d. reverse auctions

5. The concept of lifetime customer value implies that
   a. 20% of your profits come from the same 20% of your customers.
   b. customers' real requirements have not been completely satisfied.
   c. loyalty programs will be less successful than advertising campaigns.
   d. the prime customer service objective should be customer retention.

6. Good strategies for supply chain risk assessment and management might include
   a. doing stress testing through "what if" scenarios and choosing production on different continents to add flexibility.
   b. using lean practices to reduce available stock and outsourcing most processes.
   c. focusing on external disruptions, as most risks are external, and budgeting for contingencies.
   d. identifying the most serious risks and implementing passive acceptance for all but the most severe.

7. Good risk management processes for supply chain management include risk mitigation plans. These plans
   a. do not help lessen the full impact of a supply disruption.
   b. suggest increasing safety stock as the best choice to reduce risk.
   c. identify steps to take to prevent an event from occurring or lessening its impact.
   d. are generalized for categories of risk
   e. All of the above

8. A company has evaluated the risk in their supply chain and identified one risk at the starred location on the following risk assessment grid.

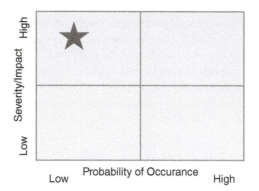

Their best strategy to manage that risk would be to
a. diversify their risk by using multiple sources.
b. hedge their risk by buying insurance.
c. mitigate their risk by increasing safety stock levels of inventory.
d. use passive acceptance of this risk as there is a very low likelihood that it will occur.

9. To estimate the trade-offs between offshoring and keeping production in the United States, supply chain managers need to conduct an evaluation for a true picture of landed costs. The evaluation should include
a. the cost of raw materials, carrying inventory, and managing product returns.
b. the local import and tax implications of locating in a given country.
c. the long-term geographic distribution of demand for your product.
d. All of the above

10. A fashion clothing manufacturer has decided to move from five finished goods warehouses around the United State to one centralized warehouse near Chicago. The company has decided to trade
a. better customer service for lower cost of transportation.
b. higher inventory for lower transportation costs.
c. higher transportation costs for lower inventory investment.
d. shorter lead time for lower transportation costs.

11. Customer relationship management (CRM) systems aid in segmenting customers using the 80/20 rule which states that
a. 20% of your sales effort should be focused on the best 80% of your customers.
b. 80% of your profit comes from 20% of your customers.
c. 20% of your business should come from new customers each year and 80% from existing customers.
d. 80% of your sales should come from existing products and 20% from new products.

12. GE switches its purchases of shelves for refrigerators from Mexico to a supplier in China, which produces them for one-third the price. For GE this is an example of

    a. increasing productivity by replacing current workers with low-quality machines.

    b. building a factory in another country to produce for that country's market.

    c. outsourcing of a component that GE uses on one of their products.

    d. increasing productivity by scaring Mexican workers into working harder.

Answers: 1(b), 2(c), 3(c), 4(d), 5(d), 6(a), 7(c), 8(b), 9(d), 10(c), 11(b), 12(c)

CASE STUDY

Plant Location Risk Assessment

A leading manufacturer and marketer of major home appliances has annual sales of over $15 billion, more than 60,000 employees, and 70 manufacturing and technology research centers around the world. The company markets major brand names to consumers globally.

The company recently announced plans to build an approximately 1 million square foot manufacturing facility for premium kitchen ranges. The new operation will support the company's commitment to delivering the world's most innovative cooking products and will be built in an energy efficient, LEED-certified facility. A 400,000 square foot distribution center is also planned.

The company is considering building the plant/distribution center in Thailand, Uruguay, or South Africa. You are the vice president of supply chain management and are evaluating these locations.

    a. Using information from the Internet, compare these locations from a supply chain perspective.

    b. Where would you recommend building the plant?

Supply Chain Technologies

9

Information technology involves the computers, telecommunications, and other devices that integrate data, equipment, personnel, and problem-solving methods in planning and controlling business activities. Information technology provides the means for collecting, storing, encoding, processing, analyzing, transmitting, receiving, and printing text, audio, or video information. A computer application program that is old and interfaces poorly with other applications but is too expensive to replace is referred to as a **legacy system**. It often runs on antiquated hardware, which is expensive to maintain. The disruption that would be caused by replacing the system can make the situation even more difficult.

Computer services sometimes referred to as **software-as-a-service (SaaS)** are provided by a third party that keeps all of the software and hardware in its place of business. A company using the service accesses the applications via the Internet. A common term for this kind of business is **cloud services**. This model allows a firm to outsource technological state-of-the-art services thus avoiding the high cost of maintaining complex software and hardware systems.

The model of how the organization operates regarding information technology is called its **information system architecture**. The model considers four factors: (1) organizational functions, (2) communication of coordination requirements, (3) data modeling needs, and (4) management and control structures. The architecture of the information system should be aligned with and match the architecture of the organization.

An **enterprise resources planning (ERP)** system forms the framework for organizing and standardizing the business processes necessary to effectively plan and control an organization. This allows the organization to use its internal knowledge to seek external advantage. Many vendors offer **modular ERP systems** that group related tasks in self-contained packages, or modules, that perform all of the tasks related to a specific function. New advances in functions can be implemented without affecting other packages or modules because of the loose coupling with other modules. One example is a multitiered architecture in which the decision models used to run the business are separated from the data management rules. Another example is a **client/server architecture** in which user interface tasks are separated from the application software.

A style of information technology design that guides all aspects of creating and using business services throughout their life cycles is the **service-oriented architecture**

(SOA). This type of design enables different computer applications to exchange data and participate in business processes, regardless of the operating systems or programming languages underlying those applications. The software that interconnects incompatible applications software and databases from various trading partners into decision-support tools such as ERP is referred to as **middleware**.

At the heart of these systems is the **database management system (DBMS)**, which is the software that organizes data and provides the mechanism for storing, maintaining, and retrieving that data on a physical medium (i.e., a database). A DBMS separates data from the application programs and people who use the data, and permits many different views of the data. A **relational database** program allows users to obtain information from two or more databases that are made up of two-dimensional arrays of data. Much more complex relationships are also available. The **data dictionary** provides a comprehensive catalogue of the specifications for the information system and includes definitions of each element of data stored in the databases used by the software systems. **Data normalization** refers to the procedure that helps to minimize data duplication and protect the database from certain logical and structural anomalies when data are combined in a relational database. To eliminate mistakes such as misspelling, missing information, and false data, **data cleansing** is done on an ongoing basis, often using automated procedures.

Due to the complexity of working directly with a database, particularly for normal users, often a **data warehouse** is setup. Data are extracted from the DBMS and placed in a simple to access repository that is used to support user-oriented decision-making applications. Often these applications are implemented using spreadsheets and specialized statistical software programs. When these repositories are set up to be accessed from the Internet, they are referred to as **portals**. Users can be given access to specific data according to their role and can aggregate and perform basic analysis according to their needs. Business data portals are often connected with a customer or supplier relationship management system. Portals can include structured data, such as ERP information, pictures, and documents. Unlike exchanges or marketplaces, portals generally can display and aggregate data without integration between application software.

To facilitate the transfer of information from a web portal, international standards are used. The following are the most common methods:

File transfer protocol (FTP) is the protocol used to transfer files over the Internet.

Hypertext markup language (HTML) is used to create web pages that permit the user to create text, hypertext links, and multimedia elements within the page. HTML is not a programming language, but a way to format text. HTML supports the design of innovative web pages with a **graphical user interface (GUI)** that uses a combination of text and graphics.

Extensible markup language (XML) facilitates direct communication among computers on the Internet. Unlike the older HTML, which provides tags giving instructions to a web browser about how to display information, XML tags give instructions to a web browser about the category of information.

Hypertext transfer protocol (HTTP) is used to move HTML and XML over the Internet. Most Internet addresses begin with *http://*.

A **local area network (LAN)** is a high-speed data communication system for linking computers, programs, and storage and graphic devices at multiple workstations distributed over a relatively small geographic area, such as a building or campus. This type of privately owned network is referred to as an **intranet** and makes use of Internet technology and applications to meet the needs of an enterprise. It resides entirely within a department or company, providing communication and access to information with web pages, similar to the Internet, and is for internal use only. When the network connection expands to a business partner's LAN, using secure information processing and Internet protocols to do business, it is referred to as an **extranet**.

To facilitate the exchange of information between business partners, internationally standardized descriptions of goods have been defined using **harmonized system classification codes**, which use a system of numbers to provide increasingly detailed classification and descriptions of items. These are important to the development of **content management applications**, which enable digital information to be exchanged online. The standardized codes allow programs written by different vendors to understand the data available from global companies and are essential to the development of efficient software solutions.

Beyond the standardization in data, the understanding of certain supply chain activities is also essential. **Supply chain event management (SCEM)** refers to supply chain management software applications, which allow users to flag the occurrence of certain supply chain events to trigger some form of alert or action within another supply chain application. SCEM can be deployed to monitor supply chain business processes such as planning, transportation, logistics, or procurement. SCEM can also be applied to supply chain business intelligence applications to alert users to any unplanned or unexpected event. An example of an event is a shipment which is scheduled to arrive outside of a targeted time window. The event would trigger a notice to a buyer/planner to take some form of action. Due to the specialized nature of some applications, a **value-added network (VAN)** might be needed to provide services beyond those provided by common data carriers.

A set of technologies that is used to collect data about objects such as inventory or plant assets and then send these data to a computer without human intervention is called **automatic identification and data capture (AIDC)** technologies. Examples include radio frequency wireless devices and terminals, bar code scanners, and smart cards.

Radio frequency identification (RFID) is a system that attaches an electronic tag to an item to store data about the item. An **active tag** is a self-powered RFID tag that broadcasts information to a receiver over a short distance. A **passive tag** is similar to the active tag but is not self-powered and must be scanned with a special reading device to access the information. The **semi-passive tag** sends out data, is self-powered, and widens its range by responding to a query from a special reader. Its range is somewhere between the active and passive tag. **Electronic product codes (EPCs)** are used with RFID tags to carry information on the product that will support warranty programs, for example.

Bar coding is a much simpler method of encoding data on a product; it can be scanned fast and accurately using simple laser devices. The **bar code** is a series of alternating bars and spaces printed or stamped on parts, containers, labels, or other media, representing encoded information about the item. Special readers scan the codes and use the data to record inventory movement.

Information exchange in supply chains is a combination of both the needed technologies previously described and the willingness to share information. Supplies chains benefit from sharing real-time information on product sales, forecasts, inventory levels, order status for tracking/tracing, performance metrics, and capacity and capability information. Sharing information can reduce costs, improve customer service levels, reduce lead times, improve profitability, increase quality levels, and enhance innovation.

Care must be taken to avoid distorting demand information as it is passed back through the chain. End customer demand information that travels back along the supply chain is often distorted as it moves back to suppliers, This phenomenon, known as the **bullwhip effect**, has been documented by a number of supply chain researchers and companies. The demand distortion is amplified as it moves away from the end customer. Forces such as demand forecast updating, order batching, promotions, fluctuating prices, and rationing and shortage gaming can cause small variances in actual consumer demand that result in progressively larger variances back through manufacturers and suppliers.

STUDY QUESTIONS

1. The "bullwhip" effect
   a. occurs only when orders are relayed from retailers to wholesalers.
   b. is when inventory is passed upstream in the supply chain, causing fluctuations at each step of the sequence.
   c. increases the costs associated with inventory in the supply chain and reduces the cost of backorders.
   d. sometimes occurs because of price changes to a product in the supply chain.

2. What is the primary way in which an ERP system accomplishes the integration of different functional areas in the company?
   a. Actually, ERP does not integrate these systems.
   b. It uses sophisticated computer hardware.
   c. It provides a shared database.
   d. It employs cutting-edge data collection devices.

3. The heart of an ERP system is the software that organizes data and provides the mechanism for storing, maintaining, and retrieving that data. This system is called a
   a. service-oriented architecture.
   b. information system architecture.
   c. data model.
   d. database management system.

4. The high-speed data communication system for linking computers is called a(n)

a. hypertext transfer protocol.

b. ethernet.

c. local area network.

d. cable network.

5. This system uses electronic tags that attach to items to store data about this item.

a. radio frequency identification

b. bar coding

c. mark sense coding

d. FM broadcasting

Answers: 1 (d), 2 (c), 3 (d), 4 (c), 5 (a)

Materials Management 10

The term *materials management* refers to the functions that support the complete cycle of material flow, from the purchase and internal control of production materials to the planning and control of work in process to the warehousing, shipping, and distribution of the finished product.

Each item in inventory is referred to as a **stock keeping unit (SKU)**. For example, a shirt in six colors and five sizes would represent 30 different SKUs. In a distribution system an item at a particular geographic location, e.g., one product stocked at the plant and at six different distribution centers would be identified with one SKU.

Inventory are those stocks of items used to support production (raw materials and work-in-process items), supporting activities (maintenance, repair, and operating supplies), and customer service (finished goods and spare parts). Inventory is carried for specific purposes, with the following being the most common:

- to anticipate expected demand,
- to act as a hedge against expected changes in price or availability,
- due to the item being produced or purchased in quantities greater than current demand (cycle stock or lot-size inventory),
- to guard against demand greater than what is expected (safety, buffer, or reserve inventory),
- to offset inventory that is in transit (transportation or pipeline inventory),
- to have on hand for service or repairs.

Demand for inventory may be dependent or independent.

Dependent demand is directly related to or derived from the bill of material (or recipe of items used) to make an end product. For example, if an item is used when a product is produced, this demand for the item is dependent. Such demands are therefore calculated and need not and should not be forecast.

Independent demand is unrelated to the demand for other items. Demand for finished goods, parts required for destructive testing, and service parts requirements are examples of independent demand.

A given inventory item may have both dependent and independent demand at any given time. For example, a part may be both the component of an assembly and sold as a service part.

Market demand is independent demand and represents the total demand that would exist within a defined customer group in a given geographical area during a particular time period given a known marketing program.

DECOUPLING AND CONSTRAINTS

The strategic positioning of inventory is an important consideration in the design and operation of a supply chain. A **buffer** is a quantity of materials waiting further processing. It can refer to raw materials, semi-finished items at hold points in a manufacturing process, or a backlog of work that is purposely maintained at a work center.

Decoupling is when a firm intentionally uses inventory buffers to enable independence between the supply and use of material. Decoupling allows the inherent fluctuations in these processes to occur without impacting the productivity of the processes. The points where the inventory buffers are located are called **decoupling points** and are identified in the product structure (for manufacturing processes) or in the distribution network. Selection of decoupling points is a strategic decision that impacts customer lead times and inventory investment. The inventory kept in these buffers is referred to as **decoupling inventory**.

A **bottleneck operation** (or simply **bottleneck**) is a facility, function, department, or resource whose capacity limits the total capacity of the process. This is significant when this capacity is less than the demand placed upon it. It is essential that a true bottleneck operation (one that is not allowing the process to meet demand) not be starved for material, so that it can operate at full utilization. A buffer is maintained prior to the process to support throughput and/or due-date performance. Other than bottlenecks, buffers can be maintained at points where parts come together for use in assemblies, at divergent points where parts supply multiple processes, and at shipping points. These buffers ensure the uninterrupted flow of material to these downstream processes.

The idea is to use buffers to help eliminate **constraints** in the supply chain. In a mathematical optimization procedure, a constraint is an equation that cannot be violated; similarly, a constraint in the supply chain is any element or factor that prevents a system from achieving a higher level of performance with respect to its goal. Constraints can be physical, such as a machine center or lack of material, but they can also be managerial, such as a policy or procedure.

INDEPENDENT DEMAND MATERIALS MANAGEMENT TERMINOLOGY

A specific vocabulary set is used when analyzing inventory management scenarios where there is a desire to stock items over time and there is significant uncertainty in future demand for the items. Examples include the inventory in a retail store, a fulfillment center that fills Internet orders, and a storeroom where spare parts and maintenance items are kept.

The **available inventory** is the **on-hand** inventory balance minus allocations, reservations, backorders, and (usually) quantities held for quality problems. This is inventory that can be used now to meet current demand.

The **inventory position** is available inventory plus the amount of inventory that is on order. This is the inventory that can be used to meet current and future demand.

The **order quantity** is the amount of the item that is obtained when inventory is replenished. Two basic types of systems are used in practice: the fixed-order quantity system and the fixed-interval order system. In a **fixed order quantity system**, the order quantity is the same each time the item is ordered. In this case when the inventory position falls to or below the reorder point or **minimum level**, the item is reordered. In a **fixed-interval order** system, orders are placed at fixed intervals of time. In this case, the order quantity is the difference between a **max-level** target and the inventory position. This amount will vary dependent on demand since the last order.

A **min-max system** is a type of order-point replenishment system that combines the ideas of the fixed-order quantity system and the fixed-interval order system. Here the minimum (min) is the order point, and the maximum (max) is the "order up to" inventory level. The order quantity is variable and is the result of the max minus inventory position. An order is recommended when inventory position is at or below the min.

The **economic order quantity** is calculated by trading off the fixed and variable costs associated with managing an item in inventory. The fixed costs are typically related to processing orders for the item. **Ordering costs** are those related to the clerical work of preparing, releasing, monitoring, and receiving orders, the physical handling of goods, inspections, and setup costs, as applicable. These costs largely depend on the number of orders that are processed. **Carrying costs** are those related to holding inventory and depend on the average amount of inventory in stock. These costs are usually defined as a percentage of the dollar value of inventory per unit of time (generally one year).

Carrying costs and ordering costs can be used in calculating order quantities. When considered over a period of time, e.g., one year, carrying cost increases as the order quantity increases, while ordering costs decrease as the order quantity increases (because the firm places fewer orders). This trade-off is the basis for the **economic order quantity** calculation.

Stockout costs are incurred when an item cannot be delivered from inventory. Those costs may include lost sales, backorder costs, expediting, and additional manufacturing and purchasing costs that are incurred to speed the delivery of the stocked-out item to the customer.

The **cycle stock** is the amount that inventory increases and decreases as the item is replenished with supplier orders and depleted with customer orders. The term *cycle* refers to the movement of inventory levels up and down over time. The other conceptual component of the item inventory is the **safety stock**, which is a cushion of extra inventory that provides protection against uncertainty in demand or in the replenishment lead time.

The **base inventory level** (or **base stock**) is made up of aggregate cycle inventory plus the safety stock inventory. It does not take into account inventory that is intentionally built in anticipation of future demand as the result of a production plan designed to increase inventory.

Anticipation inventory is additional inventory above the base inventory level to cover projected trends of increasing sales, planned sales promotion programs, seasonal fluctuations, plant shutdowns, and vacations.

Seasonal inventory (or **season stock**) is a special type of anticipation inventory built up when a firm runs at a smooth or constant production rate that is greater than current demand. The excess production is placed in inventory to be used in anticipation of later higher seasonal demand.

Seasonality is a repetitive pattern of demand from year to year (or other repeating time interval) with some periods considerably higher than others.

Obsolete inventory has met the obsolescence criteria established by the organization and will never be used or sold at full value. Disposing of this inventory may reduce a company's profit. For example, inventory that has been superseded by a new model may be declared obsolete.

In order to prioritize inventory items and sales demand for management purposes, an **ABC classification** (or **Pareto analysis**) system is sometimes used. The system uses a concept known as **Pareto's law** developed by Vilfredo Pareto, an Italian economist that states that a small percentage of a group accounts for the largest fraction of the impact, value, and so on. In an ABC classification, e.g., 20% of the inventory items (the "A" items) may constitute 80% of the inventory value. The next 30% of the items (the "B" items) are 15% of the inventory value, and the final 50% of the items (the "C" items) are only 5% of the inventory value.

Critical value analysis is a modified **ABC analysis** where a subjective metric of the criticality of an item is assigned to each item. The item may be evaluated based on it being necessary to keep a machine running in a plant, for example.

Cycle counting is an inventory accuracy audit technique where inventory is counted on a cyclic schedule rather than once a year. The cyclic schedules can be developed using an ABC classification system.

Inventory optimization software can be used to find optimal inventory strategies and policies that meet customer service levels while maximizing the return on inventory investment. Software that views inventory over several echelons, or locations, of a supply chain is particularly valuable. **Joint replenishment** opportunities involve coordinating production lot sizing and order release decisions for related items and treating them as a family of items and are particularly valuable. The objective is to achieve lower costs because of ordering, setup, shipping, and quantity discount economies. This concept applies equally to joint ordering (family contracts) and to similar part (group technology) fabrication scheduling.

Inventory turnover is the number of times that an inventory cycles, or "turns over," during the year. A frequently used method to compute inventory turnover is to divide the annual cost of goods sold by the average inventory level. For example, an annual cost of goods sold of $21 million divided by an average inventory of $3 million means that inventory turned over seven times. **Inventory velocity** is the speed with which inventory passes through an organization or supply chain at a given point in time and is measured by inventory turnover.

Inventory valuation is the worth of inventory at either its cost or its market value. Because inventory value can change with time, the age distribution of inventory is figured into the inventory valuation. Therefore, the cost value of inventory is usually computed on a **first in, first out (FIFO)** basis, **last in, last out (LIFO)** basis, or **standard cost** basis to establish the cost of goods sold.

RISK INVENTORY MODELS FOR INDEPENDENT DEMAND

(Note: A spreadsheet titled *Inventory Templates* that contains these models is available from http://www.oscm-pro.com/scp/.)

Inventory models are designed to answer questions such as how much of an item should be ordered and when an order for the item should be placed. In the case where demand is highly variable, these decisions need to consider the risk of stocking out in making these decisions.

Single-Period Decision Model

The first decision model considered is the classic **single-period problem**. This is often referred to as the newsperson problem. The newsperson has to decide how many papers to put in the sales stand outside a restaurant each morning. If the person does not put enough papers in the stand, some customers will not be able to purchase a paper, and the newsperson will lose the profit associated with these sales. On the other side, if too many papers are placed in the stand, the newsperson will have paid for papers that were not sold during the day, lowering profit for the day.

This is a very common problem. Consider the person selling T-shirts promoting a championship soccer team. This is especially difficult, since she must wait to learn what teams will be playing. The shirts can then be printed with the proper team logos. She then must estimate how many people will actually want the shirts. The shirts sold prior to the game can probably be sold at a premium price, whereas those sold after the game will need to be steeply discounted.

A way to think about this problem is to consider how much risk one is willing to take for running out of inventory. Assume that the demand is normally distributed with a mean (average) and standard deviation. If one orders the mean demand, then the risk of stock out is 50%. This means that 50% of the time demand would be greater than the mean and 50% it would be less than this amount.

If one orders the mean plus one standard deviation, then one would expect that approximately 84% of the time one would not stock out and 16% of the time one would stock out. These probabilities can be obtained using the Excel NORM.S.DIST(number of standard deviations). One can also find the number of standard deviations (the z-score) associated with a cumulative probability by using the Excel NORM.S.INV(probability) function.

For the single-period problem, the optimal stock level can be obtained through a marginal analysis and occurs at the point where the expected benefits from carrying the next unit are less than the expected costs for that unit. These benefits and costs depend on the problem.

Define costs:

C_o = Cost per Unit of Demand Overestimated

C_u = Cost per Unit of Demand Underestimated

The expected marginal cost equation is

$$P \times C_o \leq (1 - P) \times C_u$$

where P is the probability that the unit will not be sold and $1 - P$ is the probability that it will be sold.

Solving for P,

$$P \leq C_u / (C_o + C_u)$$

The equation states that one should continue to increase the size of the order so long as the probability of selling what is ordered is equal to or less than the ratio $C_u / (C_o + C_u)$.

EXAMPLE: SINGLE-PERIOD PROBLEM

A newsperson has collected data on Monday sales and determined that sales on that day average 90 papers with a standard deviation of 10 papers. The newspaper vendor pays $0.25 for each paper and sells the papers for $0.75.

Solution

In this case, the cost of overestimating demand (C_o) is the cost of paying for the paper but not selling it. This is $0.25. The cost of underestimating demand (C_u) is the loss of the profit from not selling a paper. This would be $0.75 - $0.25 = $0.50.

The critical probability where the marginal cost of overestimating demand is equal to the marginal cost of underestimating demand is

$$P \leq Cu / (Co + Cu) \leq \$0.50 / (\$0.25 + \$0.50) = 0.66666$$

This says that 66.6% of the time there should be enough papers on Monday and 33.4% of the time the stand should stock out. Converting this to a point on the cumulative probability distribution using the NORM.S.INV function in Excel, the appropriate z-score is

NORM.S.INV(.66666) = 0.430727

So given that average sales are 90 papers each Monday with a standard deviation of 10 papers, the newspaper vendor should order

Single Period Order Quantity (Q) = 90 + 0.430727 × 10 = 90 + 4.30727 = 94.30727 papers

So the newspaper person should order 94 papers and make them available on the stand on Monday morning.

MULTIPERIOD INVENTORY MODELS

It is common to keep items available so they can be immediately sold to a customer. For example, customers purchase items at a retail store directly from the stock that is kept at the store. In this case, the item is repurchased periodically to maintain the stock of the item. The systems used to manage this type of inventory are called **multiperiod inventory systems**. The key decisions that must be made in this situation are how large the order quantity should be and when the orders should be placed.

Determining the **economic order quantity (*EOQ*)** involves a trade-off of the cost of carrying the item in inventory, the cost of placing orders over the time period, and the cost of purchasing the item.

Define

PC = Purchase Cost = $D \times P(EOQ)$

Where

D = Expected Demand Over a Period of Time (typically 1 year)

EOQ = Economic Order Quantity

$P(EOQ)$ = Purchase Cost per Unit (which may depend on EOQ)

OC = Ordering Cost = $D/EOQ \times F$

where D/EOQ is the expected number of orders placed

and

F = Fixed Cost Associated with Placing an Order

CC = Carrying Cost = $I \times H$

where

H = Holding Cost to Carry One Unit for the Period of Time (typically 1 year). This is often expressed as a percent of the item value.

CS = Cycle stock = EOQ/2

where $EOQ/2$ is an estimate of average cycle stock.

SS = Safety Stock (extra inventory carried to reduce stockout risk)

I = Average Inventory = $CS + SS$

TC = Total Cost = $PC + OC + CC$

Find EOQ that minimizes TC.

EXAMPLE: ECONOMIC ORDER QUANTITY (EOQ) MODEL

Consider an item that a retailer purchases from a local supplier. Expected demand for the item over the next year is 1,000 units per week, with a standard deviation of 300 units. The supplier charges $1.50 per unit when the order quantity is less than or equal to 2,000 units. If more than 2,000 are purchased at a time, the supplier charges $1.25.

It costs the retailer approximately $50 to process each order received. This includes inspecting the order and placing the item on shelves so it can be purchased.

The carrying cost is 10% of the cost of the item. This is the cost for insurance, the value of the money tied up in inventory, and an amount reserved for pilferage of the item.

The retailer carries an extra 50 units in inventory for safety stock to protect against stocking out when the inventory level is low and a new order is being processed.

How much should the retailer order each time an order is placed to minimize the total cost or purchasing, processing orders, and carrying this item in inventory?

Solution

The yearly purchase cost for the item depends on the order quantity.

If $EOQ > 2,000$ then $PC = 1,000 \times 52 \times \$1.25 = \$65,000$

If $EOQ \leq 2,000$ then $PC = 1,000 \times 52 \times \$1.50 = \$78,000$

$OC = 1,000 \times 52 / EOQ \times \$50$

If $EOQ > 2,000$ then $CC = (EOQ/2 + 50) \times \$1.25 \times 0.1$

If $EOQ \leq 2,000$ then $CC = (EOQ/2 + 50) \times \$1.50 \times 0.1$

$TC = PC + OC + CC$

Using the Excel Solver, find EOQ to minimize TC.

$EOQ = 6,449.807$ or $6,450$ units

$TC = \$65,000 + \$403.1128 + \$409.3629 = \$65,812.48$

A data table can be constructed in Excel using a Data Table (see Appendix A) to show how total cost (TC) varies as a function of the order quantity (Q). The following chart was developed using this tool:

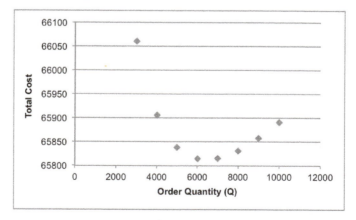

Note that the total cost associated with order quantities between 6,000 and 7,000 units does not vary greatly. In that range the total cost curve is fairly flat.

Rarely would a firm actually request the economic order quantity; rather, the number is used as guide to the range of order quantities that are economically reasonable.

When quantity discounts are not present, the economic order quantity can be quickly calculated using the following Excel formula:

EOQ = SQRT (2 × D × F / CC)

Given an economic order quantity that is obtained by minimizing cost, the next issue with managing an item is when to place the order. In general, there are two approaches that are used in practice. The first approach is to frequently monitor the inventory level and place an order when it gets down to a low and critical level. Recall that this low level is called the reorder point or min-level. In this case a fixed order quantity guided by the economic order quantity would be purchased. This type of system is often referred to as a **fixed order quantity** system.

The second approach is to monitor the inventory level with a much less frequent but specific interval of time. At the end of each of these time intervals, an order is placed to replenish inventory up to a max-level. For example, the firm might place orders for a group of items supplied by a specific vendor every four weeks. This may allow more efficient processing and shipping of the group order. This type of system is often referred to as a **fixed-interval order** system that was described earlier.

Details associated with the precise calculation of the maximum and minimum levels are beyond the scope of this text, but what is desired is a managerial level understanding of the aggregate operation of these systems, and its impact on **average inventory investment**.

Safety Stock in Inventory Models

With both types of ordering systems, safety stock is used to reduce the risk of stockouts. This risk is due to the uncertainty in demand over the periods of time when the item is reviewed and also the time that it takes to replenish the item. For example, if an item is only reviewed once every four weeks (this is called the **review period**), there is the possibility that the item may stock out during those four weeks. Further, if it takes another two weeks to receive a new order from the supplier (this is called the suppler **lead time**), there is risk based on the uncertainty in demand over this entire six-week period. If, on the other hand, the item is reviewed every day by an automated system, then the risk is based on the uncertainty in demand over that one day review period plus the two week supplier lead time period.

Safety stock should be carried in the system to reduce the risk of stocking out over the **protection interval**. The **protection interval** is the sum of the review period plus the lead time. This safety stock can be defined as a fixed amount, e.g., average demand over 3 week periods, or based on a statistical calculation that uses the demand forecast. In the following, the statistical approach is explained:

d = Expected Demand Over One Period

STDEV(d) = Standard Deviation of Demand Over One Period

R = Review Period

L = Lead Time

D = Expected Demand Over the Protection Interval = $d \times (R + L)$

STDEV(D) = SQRT($R+L$) × STDEV(d) (assumes demand is independent each period)

RISK = Probability of *Not* Stocking Out = 1 − Probability of Stocking Out

SS = Safety Stock = NORM.S.INV(RISK) × STDEV(D)

EXAMPLE: STATISTICAL SAFETY STOCK CALCULATION

Consider an item where the review period (R) is one week and supplier lead time (L) is three weeks.

The expected weekly demand is 1,000 units with a standard deviation of 100 units. The firm expects to order the item about 50 times over the next year and would only be willing to stock out during one of these order cycles. How much safety stock should be carried on the item?

Solution

R = 1 week

L = 3 weeks

D = 1,000 × (1 + 3) = 4,000 units

STDEV(D) = SQRT(1 + 3) × STDEV(d) = 2 × 100 = 200 units

RISK = 1- (1 stockout /50 cycles) = 0.98 (98% probability of not stocking out)

SS = NORM.S.INV(.98) × 200 = 410.7498

So 411 units of safety stock should be carried.

At this point, **average inventory** can be estimated based on the expected order quantity (Q) and the safety stock (SS) carried on an item. The average is equal to 50% of the expected order quantity plus the safety stock. The rationale is that as supplier orders replenish the inventory for an item and customer orders deplete inventory, the average inventory cycle will be 50% of the order quantity. This is called **cycle stock**. At the end of each cycle, inventory is expected to drop down to the safety stock level (50% of the time it is expected to end at a level greater than the safety stock, and 50% of the time it will drop into the safety stock).

Where

Q = Order Quantity (This may be an average value or a fixed amount, depending on the system.)

SS = Safety Stock (This could be based on statistics or a fixed amount.)

$I_{Average}$ = $Q/2$ + SS

Finally, an estimate of yearly **inventory turns** for the item can be calculated by taking the expected yearly demand and dividing by the average inventory.

IT = Inventory Turn = $D_{Year} / I_{Average}$

Managerially, this is useful for estimating the amount of inventory and the impact this has on inventory investment.

Another useful measure is **weeks of supply**. This is the amount of inventory on hand measured as a number of weeks' worth of inventory. This value is the inverse of inventory turn, expressed in number of weeks.

WS = Weeks of Supply = 52 weeks/IT

EXAMPLE: AVERAGE INVENTORY AND INVENTORY TURN CALCULATIONS

Consider an item where the order quantity is 6,000 units and the safety stock is 1,000 units. The expected demand for the item over the next year is 26,000 units.

What is the average inventory for the item and the expected inventory turn?

Solution

Q = 6,000 units

SS = 1,000 units

$I_{Average}$ = 6,000/2 + 1,000 = 4,000 units

IT = 26,000/4,000 = 6.5 times per year

WS = 52/6.5 = 8 weeks

INVENTORY PROBLEMS

1) The local supermarket buys lettuce each day to ensure really fresh produce. Each morning any lettuce that is left from the previous day is sold to a dealer who resells it to farmers who use it to feed their animals. This week the supermarket can buy fresh lettuce for $4.00 a box. The lettuce is sold for $10.00 a box, and the dealer that sells the old lettuce is willing to pay $1.50 a box. Past history says that tomorrow's demand for lettuce averages 250 boxes with a standard deviation of 34 boxes. How many boxes of lettuce should the supermarket purchase tomorrow?

2) Next week, Air France has a flight from Rome to Zagreb that will be booked to capacity. The airline knows from past history that an average of 25 customers (with a standard deviation of 15) cancels their reservation or do not show for the flight. Net income from a ticket on the flight is $125. If the flight is overbooked, the airline has a policy of

getting the customer on the next available flight and giving the person a free round-trip ticket on a future flight. The cost of this free round-trip ticket averages $250. Air France considers the cost of flying the plane from Rome to Zagreb a sunk cost. By how many seats should Air France overbook the flight?

3) A particular raw material is available to a company at three different prices, depending on the size of the order: (1) less than 100 pounds is $20/pound, (2) 100 pounds to 1,000 pounds is $19/pound, and (3) more than 1,000 pounds is $18/pound.

> The cost to place an order is $40. Annual demand is 3,000 units. Holding (or carrying cost) is 25% of the material price. What is the economic order quantity for the material?

4) Daily demand for a certain product is normally distributed with a mean of 100 and a standard deviation of 15. The supplier is reliable and maintains a constant lead time of 5 days. The cost of placing an order is $10, and the cost of holding inventory is $0.50/unit per year. The company has a goal of not stocking out 90% of the order cycles. Assume that sales occur over 360 days each year.

> a) Calculate the optimal order quantity for the item.

> b) Assuming that the item is reviewed every day, calculate the required safety stock for the item given the 5-day supplier lead time.

> c) How much inventory would the company have on average?

> d) How many weeks of supply?

5) Nikola's Pizza orders all of its pepperoni, olives, anchovies, and mozzarella cheese directly from Italy. A Croatian distributor stops by every four weeks to take orders. Because the orders are shipped directly from Italy, they take three weeks to arrive. Nikola's uses an average of 150 pounds of pepperoni each week, with a standard deviation of 30 pounds. Nikola's prides itself on offering only the best-quality ingredients and a high level of service, so it wants to ensure a 98% probability of not stocking out on pepperoni.

> a) On average, how much pepperoni do you expect Nikola's to have on-hand?

> b) How many weeks of supply is this?

STUDY QUESTIONS

1. If Westside Manufacturing has an average aggregate inventory value of $100,000, assets worth $600,000, net margin of 10%, and cost of goods sold of $450,000, which of these is their inventory turnover?
   a. 19.23
   b. 4.5
   c. 0.8654
   d. 0.2222

2. You are the operations manager of a company which has a "weeks of supply"
   metric of 15 weeks. Are you doing well or performing poorly?
   a. This is good; you are doing well.
   b. This is bad; you need to improve performance.
   c. You don't know; it depends on past performance and industry best practice.
   d. You don't know; you need to calculate inventory turnover to tell.

3. If Westside Manufacturing's average aggregate inventory value is $1,200,000
   and cost of goods sold is $600,000, which of the following is their weeks of
   supply based on working 52 weeks a year?
   a. 1,040
   b. 606
   c. 104
   d. 60.6

4. An automobile manufacturer needs 8 brake pads for each car that it produces
   on the assembly line. This is an example of what kind of demand?
   a. market demand
   b. modular demand
   c. independent demand
   d. dependent demand

5. When a firm uses inventory to enable independence between the operations of
   a supply chain, this is called
   a. decoupling.
   b. postponement.
   c. outsourcing.
   d. strategic positioning.

6. A bottleneck is important to recognize in a process because it
   a. cannot operate at full utilization.
   b. has less capacity than the demand placed on it.
   c. has uninterrupted flow and needs to be slowed.
   d. is the source of many defects.

7. The purpose of safety stock is to
   a. replace failed units with good ones.
   b. eliminate the possibility of a stockout.
   c. eliminate the likelihood of a stockout due to erroneous inventory tally.
   d. control the likelihood of a stockout due to the variability of demand during
      lead time.

8. The new manager of production at a company uses EOQ to determine lot sizes. The manager has ordered all departments to work on reducing the cost to set up (this reduces the fixed cost to make an order) the machines so that the company can reduce inventory costs. Is this strategy correct and why/why not?

   a. No. Reducing order setup costs has no impact on inventory costs in EOQ calculations.

   b. Yes. Reducing order setup costs makes the optimal EOQ larger, which reduces inventory costs.

   c. No. Reducing order setup costs makes the optimal EOQ larger, which increases inventory costs.

   d. Yes. Reducing order setup costs makes the optimal EOQ smaller, which reduces inventory costs.

9. The assistant manager of Home and Hearth is reviewing the current ordering policy of the store's best-selling frying pan. Their current ordering policy is to order 125 units per order. If the optimal ordering quantity as calculated by the simple EOQ model was 175 units per order, which of the following statements are correct with respect to the costs incurred by the company?

   a. If the manager orders the EOQ lot size rather than the current lot size, the annual holding cost will increase.

   b. If the manager orders the EOQ lot size rather than the current lot size, the annual setup cost will increase.

   c. If the manager orders according to the EOQ lot size, the annual purchase price of the frying pans ordered will increase.

   d. a and c

Answers: 1 (b), 2 (c), 3 (c), 4 (d), 5 (a), 6 (b), 7 (d), 8 (d), 9 (a)

Supply Chain Inventory Planning

11

WAREHOUSE INVENTORIES

Warehouse management systems (WMS) are used to manage all the processes that a warehouse carries out. These processes include receiving, picking, and shipping of material stored in a warehouse.

Inventory in the transportation network and the distribution system, including the flow through intermediate stocking points is call **pipeline stock**. The flow time through the pipeline has a major effect on the amount of inventory required in the pipeline. Factors that impact flow time involve order transmission, order processing, scheduling, shipping, transportation, receiving, stocking, review time, and other time-consuming activities.

> **Distribution inventory** is material, usually spare parts and finished goods, located in the distribution system, e.g., in warehouses, in-transit between warehouses and the consumer.

> **In-transit** or **transportation inventory** is material moving between two or more locations, usually separated geographically, e.g., finished goods being shipped from a plant to a distribution center.

Cross-docking is the concept of packing products on incoming shipments to warehouses so they can be easily sorted for outgoing shipments based on final destination. The items are moved from the incoming vehicle docking point to the outgoing vehicle docking point without being stored in inventory at the warehouse. Cross-docking reduces inventory investment and storage space requirements.

Cross-docking could be used in a food supply chain for a ready-to-eat cereal such as Cheerios. A full semitrailer load of cases of cereal arrives at the customer's distribution center. Rather than put the Cheerios on the shelf, the truck is unloaded, and the cases are put on a conveyor system and delivered to outgoing trucks that are headed to a specific store. No one store can handle a full truck load of Cheerios but putting the cases on a shelf first before sending them out to stores adds extra handling cost and adds no value. Every time a product is touched, e.g., taking it on and off the shelf, cost is added to the product. Alternatively, shipping less-than-truckload shipments to each store would likely add significant transportation costs.

Consigned stock or **inventory**, usually refers to finished goods that are in the possession of customers, dealers, agents, and so on, but remain the property of the manufacturer by agreement with those in possession.

Fair-share quantity logic is a mathematical way to allocate inventory where the objective is to maximize customer service from the limited available inventory. Typically the idea is to give to each customer an amount so that the expected service levels are the same for all customers.

Distribution requirements planning (DRP) is logic used for planning warehouse inventory needs. It is often used to determine when to replenish inventory at branch warehouses. A time-phased order point approach is used where the planned orders at the branch warehouse level are "exploded" via Material Requirements Planning (MRP) logic (see the following section) to become the requirements on the supplying source. In the case of multilevel distribution networks, this explosion process can continue down through the various levels of regional warehouses (master warehouse, factory warehouse, etc.) and serve as input to the master production schedule (see the following section). Demand on the supplying sources is recognized as dependent, and standard MRP logic applies. More generally, replenishment inventory calculations may be based on other planning approaches such as period order quantities or "replace exactly what was used," rather than being limited to the time-phased order point approach just described.

FACTORY INVENTORIES

Material requirements planning (MRP) is the basic set of techniques that uses bill of material data, inventory data, and the master production schedule (MPS) to calculate requirements for materials. It makes recommendations to release replenishment orders for material when it is needed. Further, because it is time-phased, it makes recommendations to reschedule open orders when due dates and need dates are not aligned. Time-phased MRP begins with the items listed on the MPS and determines (1) the quantity of all components and materials required to fabricate those items and (2) the date that the components and material are required. Time-phased MRP is accomplished by exploding the bill of material, adjusting for inventory quantities on hand or on order, and offsetting the net requirements by the appropriate lead times.

Master planning is the process used in a factory for integrating the demand placed on the factory through orders or forecast demand; along with the production and resource plan. Master planning includes master scheduling (where the master schedule and the rough-cut capacity plan are made).

The **master production schedule (MPS)** reflects the anticipated build schedule for those items assigned to the master scheduler. The master scheduler maintains this schedule, and in turn, it becomes a set of planning numbers that drives material requirements planning. It represents what the company plans to produce expressed in specific configurations, quantities, and dates. The master production schedule is not a sales item forecast that represents a statement of demand. The master production schedule must take into account the forecast, the production plan, and other important considerations such as backlog, availability of material and capacity, and management policies and goals.

The **planning horizon** is the amount of time a plan extends into the future. For a master schedule, this is normally set to cover a minimum of the cumulative lead time plus time for lot sizing low-level components and for capacity changes of primary work centers or of key suppliers. For longer-term plans, the planning horizon must be long enough to permit any needed additions to capacity.

The **production forecast** is the projected level of customer demand for a feature (option, accessory, etc.) of a make-to-order or an assemble-to-order product.

The **mix forecast** is the expected proportion of products that will be sold within a given product family, or the proportion of options offered within a product line. Product and option mix as well as aggregate product families must be forecasted. Even though the appropriate level of units is forecasted for a given product line, an inaccurate mix forecast can create material shortages and inventory problems.

When one plant in a company needs a part or product that is produced by another plant or division within the same organization, this is known as **interplant demand** or **transfer**. Although it is not a customer order, it is usually handled by the master production scheduling system in a similar manner.

A **demand time fence (DTF)** is that point in time before which the forecast is no longer included in total demand and projected available inventory calculations; before this point, only customer orders are considered. Beyond this point, total demand is a combination of actual orders and forecasts, depending on the forecast consumption technique chosen. In some contexts, the demand time fence may correspond to that point in the future inside which changes to the master schedule must be approved by an authority higher than the master scheduler. Note, however, that customer orders may still be promised inside the demand time fence without higher authority approval if there are quantities available. Beyond the demand time fence, the master scheduler may change the MPS within the limits of established rescheduling rules, without the approval of higher authority.

The **cumulative lead time** is the longest planned length of time to accomplish the activity in question. It is found by reviewing the lead time for each bill of material path below the item; whichever path adds up to the greatest number defines cumulative lead time.

The term **cycle time** is used differently, depending on the context. In industrial engineering when referring to a discrete manufacturing process such as an assembly line, this is the time between the completions of two discrete units of production. For example, the cycle time of motors assembled at a rate of 120 per hour would be 30 seconds. In materials management, it refers to the length of time from when material enters a production facility until it exits. Many have adopted the term **throughput time** in the materials management setting to avoid the confusion.

Final assembly schedule (FAS) is the schedule of end items to finish the product for specific customers' orders in a make-to-order or assemble-to-order environment.

Load leveling or **capacity smoothing** is the spreading of orders out in time or rescheduling operations so that the amount of work to be done in sequential time periods tends to be distributed evenly and is achievable. Although both material and labor are ideally level loaded, specific businesses and industries may load to one or the other exclusively (e.g., service industries).

The **level schedule** in traditional materials management is a production schedule or master production schedule that generates material and labor requirements that are spread over time as evenly as possible. Finished goods inventories buffer the production system against seasonal demand. In JIT, this is a schedule, usually constructed monthly, in which each day's customer demand is scheduled to be built on the day it will be shipped. A level schedule is the output of the load-leveling process.

The **order backlog** comprises customer orders received but not yet shipped. A **backorder** is an unfilled customer order where the commitment to the order has not been made. For example, the due date and/or the specified order quantity has not been met. The intent is that these commitments will eventually be met in the future. A **stock-out** occurs when actual demand exists, but it will not be met in the future because material is not available.

An **assembly** or **manufacturing order** authorizes a department to put components together to produce something (either a product or a subassembly) as part of an assembly or pure manufacturing process. Sometime these are referred to as **work orders**.

A bill of material (BOM) or **assembly parts list** is a listing of all the subassemblies, intermediates, parts, and raw materials that go into a parent assembly showing the quantity of each required to make a good. The BOM is used in conjunction with the master production schedule to determine the items for which purchase requisitions and production orders must be released. A variety of display formats exist for BOMs, including the single-level, indented, modular (planning), transient, matrix, and costed BOM. The bill of material may also be called the *formula*, *recipe*, or *ingredients list* in certain process industries.

A **modular BOM** is often used in companies where the product has many optional features (e.g., **assemble-to-order** companies such as automobile manufacturers). In this case, the listing is of subassemblies that are mixed and matched for the final assembly of the product.

A **repetitive manufacturing** environment is one where the same, or a very similar item, is produced over and over again. Work orders are no longer necessary and production scheduling and control are based on production rates.

In MRP, the **net requirements** for a part or an assembly are derived as a result of applying gross requirements and allocations against inventory on hand, scheduled receipts, and safety stock. Net requirements, lot -sized and offset for lead time, become **planned orders**.

The **projected available inventory** is the running sum of on-hand inventory minus requirements plus scheduled receipts and planned orders.

Available-to-promise (ATP) is inventory that is available or will be in the future, but that has not yet been allocated to meet specific customer orders. In some contexts the process for committing this inventory and the available capacity for making the item is referred to as **capable-to-promise (CTP)** logic.

PLANNING AND SCHEDULING

Advanced planning and scheduling or **advanced planning systems (APS)** deal with the analysis and planning of logistics and manufacturing during short-, intermediate-, and long-term time periods. APS describes any computer program that uses advanced mathematical algorithms or logic to perform optimization or simulation on finite-capacity scheduling, sourcing, capital planning, resource planning, forecasting, demand management, and others. These systems use techniques that simultaneously consider a range of constraints and business rules to provide real-time planning and scheduling, decision support, ATP, and CTP capabilities. APS often generates and evaluates multiple scenarios thus providing the user with decision options to consider. Management then selects one scenario to use as the "official plan." The five main components of APS systems are (1) demand planning, (2) production planning, (3) production scheduling, (4) distribution planning, and (5) transportation planning.

The systems incorporate **feedback**, which is the flow of information back into the control system so that actual performance can be compared with planned performance. The systems measure the difference between the expected (budgeted or planned) value and the actual value for such items as demand, production rates, and transit times. Using this feedback the system employs **optimization** techniques to achieve the best possible solution to a problem in terms of a specified objective function.

A common class of optimization techniques is based on **mathematical programming**, which address the general problem of optimizing a function of several variables subject to a number of constraints. If the function and constraints have linear relationships between the variables and a subset of the constraints restricts the variables to be nonnegative, a **linear programming** problem exists. Linear programming solves linear optimization problems through minimization or maximization of a linear function subject to linear constraints. For example, in blending gasoline and other petroleum products, many intermediate distillates may be available. Prices and octane ratings as well as upper limits on capacities of input materials that can be used to produce various grades of fuel are given. The goal is to blend the various inputs in such a way that (1) cost will be minimized (profit will be maximized), (2) specified optimum octane ratings will be met, and (3) the need for additional storage capacity will be reduced.

Another useful technique is **simulation**, where representative data are used to reproduce in a mathematical model various conditions that are likely to occur in the actual performance of a system. It is frequently used to test the behavior of a system under different operating policies. Simulation can be used to perform what-if evaluations of alternative plans to answer a question such as, "Can we do it?" If yes, the simulation can then be run in the financial mode to help answer the question, "Do we really want to?"

The **business plan** for an ongoing business is a statement of long-range strategy and includes projections of revenue, cost, and profit. The plan is accompanied by budgets, a projected balance sheet, and a cash flow (source and application of funds) statement. A business plan is usually stated in terms of dollars and grouped by product family. The business plan is translated into synchronized tactical functional plans through the production planning process (or the sales and operations planning process). Although frequently stated in different terms (dollars versus units), these tactical plans should agree with each other and with the business plan.

The process to develop tactical plans starts with the **sales and operations planning (S&OP)** process. The process is designed to provide management the ability to strategically direct its businesses to achieve competitive advantage on a continuous basis by integrating customer-focused marketing plans for new and existing products with the management of the supply chain. The process brings together all the plans for the business (sales, marketing and development, manufacturing, sourcing, and financial) into one integrated set of plans. It is performed at least once a month and is reviewed by management at an aggregate (product family) level. The process must reconcile all supply, demand, and new-product plans at both the detail and aggregate levels and tie into the business plan. It is the definitive statement of the company's plans for the near to intermediate term, covering a horizon sufficient to plan for resources and to support the annual business planning process. Executed properly, the sales and operation planning process links the strategic plan for the business with its execution and reviews performance measurements for continuous improvement.

Depending on characteristics of the business, the tactical strategy for matching the output of the production system with demand can take on some fundamentally different characteristics. The **chase production method** involves planning production so that a stable inventory level is maintained by varying production to meet demand. A different approach is the **level production method** that maintains a stable production rate while varying inventory levels to meet demand. Another approach involves **subcontracting** or outsourcing production work to another manufacturer. Companies may combine the chase, level, and subcontracting approaches based on cost tradeoffs and future demand uncertainty. These tradeoffs can be modeled mathematically and studied using optimization and simulation techniques.

Similar to the production planning approach described previously, a **transportation management system (TMS)** is used to plan the movement of goods through a supply chain. A TMS manages the operation of transportation systems including deciding on modes of transportation (e.g., water, rail, truck, air, pipeline), planning imports and exports, planning and controlling fleet service activities, and load planning and optimization.

STUDY QUESTION

1. Cross-docking in distribution centers involves
   a. having multiple locations for the same item in the warehouse.
   b. having multiple docks to load items in and out of trucks.
   c. a docking system that allows trucks to unload parallel to the dock rather than from the rear of the truck.
   d. a new type of docking system where the docks lie at right angles to each other.
   e. moving product from incoming trucks directly to outgoing trucks.

Answer: 1(e)

The E-Game Company

Late one Friday afternoon, George Heller was trying to formulate an approach to his job as finished goods warehouse manager for the E-Game Company. As finished goods warehouse manager at the E-Game Company, he had the responsibility for managing the inventories of the company's entire line of computer games. He decided to study in detail a representative product, The Big Game, as the basis for his plans.

Background

One of the important elements of communication in the company was the Monday morning management meeting. During this time, the key people of the company got together and discussed current problems, production plans, and new product ideas. It was during these meetings that Mr. Heller was to place replenishment orders for products which were getting low in inventory. These orders were given directly to the production manager, Roger Blake.

The E-Game Company's production process was quite simple. The production manager received all replenishment orders at the Monday meeting and forwarded them to a nearby DVD duplication company where the DVDs were prepared during the early part of the week. During the latter part of the week and sometimes on the weekend, the games were assembled and boxed at the E-Game Company plant using part-time help. The completed games were packed in cases and transferred to the finished goods warehouse on Monday morning of the following week. In discussing the situation with the production manager, Mr. Heller was assured that, at least for the foreseeable future, there would be no limitations on production capacity.

In his discussion with other people in the company, Mr. Heller found that when the company didn't have enough inventory to fill a customer's order, the amount by which they were short was lost. That is, the company was not able to back order the shortage, and its customers apparently filled their requirements with competitive products.

In discussing the finished goods inventory with other officers, Mr. Heller found that space was not a critical problem. The finished goods warehouse had been designed with space for expansion into new product lines should the company so desire. Capital, however, was a continual problem for the company because of a rapid growth in the product line. Mr. Heller felt he could use the Friday night inventory balance to determine the inventory level for capital investment purposes.

The Big Game

Mr. Heller turned his attention to The Big Game as a representative company product. His predecessor had left him no information on the management of the inventories, but there were two years of demand history for The Big Game (see next page). In discussing

The E-Game Company: Past Demand for The Big Game (Cases per week)

Week	Two Years Ago	Last Year	Week	Two Years Ago	Last Year
1	25	19	26	22	19
2	18	26	27	19	26
3	21	17	28	26	22
4	21	18	29	18	28
5	21	26	30	18	28
6	17	17	31	19	18
7	19	17	32	21	17
8	18	17	33	18	16
9	20	22	34	19	16
10	19	22	35	20	17
11	25	18	36	18	18
12	24	17	37	19	17
13	20	19	38	23	21
14	19	18	39	23	26
15	19	19	40	18	24
16	17	18	41	17	18
17	18	22	42	17	18
18	23	20	43	23	19
19	20	17	44	20	23
20	19	22	45	19	18
21	23	26	46	17	25
22	18	17	47	27	23
23	19	17	48	20	18
24	19	18	49	28	16
25	19	22	50*	22	17

*The Gaming Company took a two-week vacation each summer.

The Big Game with the salesmen, Mr. Heller found that it was a relatively stable item in the company's product line and that it had no seasonal sales peaks. The salesmen were in agreement that conditions in the current year would not be different from those of past years and past demand would be a good indication of what to expect in the future.

In reviewing the costs of The Big Game, Mr. Heller found that the DVD duplication company charged a fixed amount of $9 for each order to cover the costs of setting up their duplicating equipment and delivering the finished DVDs to the company. There

Sample Evaluation Sheet for the E-Game Company

Week Number	1	2	3	4	5	6	7	8	9	10
Monday Morning Inventory	43[1]	53[4]	35	14	100[6]	79	62	43	25	40
Week's Demand	25	18	21	21	21	17	19	18	20	19
Friday Night Inventory	18	35	14	–7	79	62	43	25	5	21
Number Ordered	35	0	0	100	0	0	0	0	35	0
Setup Costs ($9 per order)	9.00[2]	0	0	9.00	0	0	0	0	9.00	0
Inventory Costs ($0.1 per case)	1.80[3]	3.50	1.40	0	7.90	6.20	4.30	2.50	.50	2.10
Shortage Costs ($1 per case)	0	0	0	7.00[5]	0	0	0	0	0	0
Total Costs for Week	10.80	3.50	1.40	16.00	7.90	6.20	4.30	2.50	9.50	2.10
Cumulative Cost from Last Week	--	10.80	14.30	15.70	31.70	39.60	45.80	50.10	52.60	62.10
Cumulative Cost to Date	10.80	14.30	15.70	31.70	39.60	45.80	50.10	52.60	62.10	64.20

Notes: [1]Opening balance as of next Monday, [2]Cost of placing the order for 35 cases, [3]Friday night inventory at $0.10 per case, [4]Friday night inventory of 18 plus order of 35, [5]Short 7 cases at $1 per case, [6]The order of 100 only since the 7 cases short are not back ordered

were no comparable fixed costs for the assembly of the completed games at the plant. The management of the company had estimated that it cost $1 per case for each case short on a customer's order. This represented both the loss of profit on that case and some measure of lost goodwill.

An estimate of the opportunity cost of capital and direct costs of carrying inventory had been made, and for The Big Game this amounted to $0.10 per week per case. Since he had decided that the Friday night inventory was the relevant inventory, Mr. Heller decided to use that as the inventory level against which he would assess the $0.10 cost. There was a balance of 43 cases of The Big Game in inventory, and he hadn't placed a replenishment order in the last management meeting. He next turned his attention to investigating different methods for managing the inventories and to see if he needed to place an order on the following Monday.

Simulation

Mr. Heller thought one approach to the evaluation of different alternatives for managing the inventories would be simulation using a spreadsheet. He devised a spreadsheet on which he could evaluate different alternatives. At the top of page 115 is a printout of one of his evaluations.

In compiling this example, Mr. Heller used the sales history as a representative demand sequence.

Assignment

1. Replicate Mr. Heller's spreadsheet using Excel. Design the spreadsheet so that the demand and orders can be changed manually. (Note: A spreadsheet template titled *E-Game Company* is available on http://www.oscm-pro.com/scp/.)
2. Develop decision logic to aid Mr. Heller in making his Monday morning decision. One suggestion might be to determine the number of units that he would be comfortable with on Monday morning without placing an order. When an order is needed, determine how many cases should be ordered.
3. Program your decision logic into the spreadsheet, so that if demand is changed orders are automatically initiated.
4. Test your logic by using the following demand stream: 18 18 17 25 21 19 18 25 20 19, with a starting inventory of 43 cases. What is the total cumulative cost over the 10 weeks?

Integrative Supply Chain Analysis

12

So far, this book has considered everything as an independent decision. Now consider the fact that these are not independent but are interconnected. Demand characteristics, for example, are dependent on how customers are segmented. Warehouse locations are dependent on this partitioning, and drive transportation and inventory costs. Plant location drives the direct cost of the product as well as transportation costs.

Other than these quantifiable costs, there are other considerations. These include issues of speed related to lead times, flexibility in the relative size of orders, currency risk, taxes, and local market demand response.

Performing an integrative supply chain analysis can be organized in six major steps: (1) Define the project, (2) scope the analysis, (3) select appropriate scenarios, (4) identify relevant measures, (5) make simplifying assumptions, and (6) sensitivity analysis.

Step 1. Define the project. Each project is developed to make a specific decision. For example, should the company use a new process, build a new warehouse, outsource to a new manufacturer? A clear statement of why the project is being considered and what decision needs to be made is essential to a successful supply chain analysis project.

Step 2. Scope the analysis. This requires defining the boundaries of the analysis by identifying which elements of the system will be considered and which will not. The idea is to limit the analysis to as small a project as possible where the results can be extrapolated to the system as a whole.

> Often, in the context of supply chains, the analysis is limited to a single item or a small group of items. Each item used in the study should be representative of a larger group of items, which allows the result to be scaled to the real situation. Often the item(s) would be selected based on demand (high or low) or seasonality. It is important to capture those characteristics that will make the analysis useful for making the decision involved.

> Another consideration in scoping the project is identifying the resources that will be impacted by the decision. What plant, warehouse, or transportation resource needs to be considered? Resources that generate significant cost and are impacted by the potential decision need to be included in the project.

Step 3. Select appropriate scenarios. A project generally starts by analyzing a base case that captures the current situation. This base case is the point of comparison relative to performance measures such as cost and delivery speed. The model used in the analysis must meaningfully capture this base case.

> After identifying the base case, changes are made to the base case data. Initially, scenarios are identified that represent only a single change to the base case. For example, the order quantity is increased or the supplier is switched, while holding everything else in the system the same. After these single-change scenarios are identified, then scenarios can be addressed that involve combinations of changes.

> Scenarios are selected that will shed light on the impact of the proposed changes to the system. Learning what change has the largest impact and how combinations of changes interact, for example, is important.

Step 4. Identify relevant measures. A relevant measure is one that will change significantly based on the decision. Typically these measures relate to cost. Service response and delivery speed are also often important measures in supply chain analysis. Costs that do not change should be considered "sunk costs" and need not be modeled.

> It is important to have a general idea of how these measures should change relative to one another prior to actually developing the model. For example, if a fixed cost goes up, what variable costs should go down? Understanding these relationships is important for validating that the model is coded correctly and more generally understanding the problem.

Step 5. Make simplifying assumptions. It is important in the analysis to keep the model as simple as possible while keeping its relevance. Assuming that demand is normally distributed, for example, can often make the model much simpler. Also, assuming linear relationships between costs and system characteristics, e.g., transportation cost and distance traveled can make the model much easier to manage. Another idea is to just model a small subset of the system, rather than the whole system, e.g., modeling material flow in North America or Europe, rather than the whole world.

Step 6. Sensitivity analysis. The robustness of a decision is an important consideration. Since the model is an abstraction of the real situation and not necessarily perfectly accurate, it is important to understand how sensitive the decision is to the assumptions made in the model. For example, what if labor cost was incorrect by 30%? Would the same decision still be made? What if transportation costs were incorrect by 10%? Would this impact the decision? Key parameters in the model need to be identified and the sensitivity of these parameters should be tested as part of the project analysis.

Performing an integrative supply chain analysis is as much an art as it is an exercise in quantitative modeling. There is much judgment related to making all the decisions related to scoping and measures that have a direct impact on the usefulness of the analysis. It is often good to start small with a simple model and only the most basic relationships. Much can be learned from a simple model. The model can always be expanded according to the need to make the model more relevant.

A type of problem appropriate for supply chain analysis is one where a company has customers in multiple locations and has a number of warehouse locations that could provide product to each customer. Available information might include

customer locations;

order size and frequency from each customer;

transport modes and costs;

warehouse/distribution center size, location, resources, costs, etc.;

service level requirements;

factory locations; and

ports of entry for imported products.

This information would be modeled with the goal of assigning customers to the most cost-effective distribution center.

CASE STUDY

US Electronics

(Note: The data for this case is in a spreadsheet titled *US Electronics* that is available at http://www.oscm-pro.com/scp/.)

US Electronics (USE) is an American manufacturer of electronic equipment. The company has a single manufacturing facility in San Jose, California. USE distributes its products through five warehouses located in Atlanta, Boston, Chicago, Dallas, and Los Angeles. In the current distribution system, the United States is partitioned into five major markets, each of which is served by a single regional warehouse. Customers, typically retail outlets, receive items directly from the regional warehouse in their market. That is, in the current distribution system, each customer is assigned to a single market and receives deliveries from one regional warehouse.

The warehouses receive items from the manufacturing facility. Typically it takes two weeks to satisfy an order placed by any of the regional warehouses. The warehouses use a reorder point system for controlling inventory. Currently, USE provides their customers with a probability of not stocking out of 90%.

In recent years, USE has seen a significant increase in competition and huge pressure from their customers to improve service levels and reduce costs. To this end, USE would like to consider an alternative distribution strategy in which the five regional warehouses are replaced with a single central warehouse that will be in charge of all the customer orders. This warehouse should be one of the existing warehouses. The company CEO insists that whatever distribution strategy is used, USE will design the strategy so that the customer probability of not stocking out is increased to about 97%.

To perform a rigorous analysis, you have identified a typical product, Product A. The first table provides historical data that includes weekly demand for this product for the last 12 weeks in each of the market areas. An order placed by a warehouse to the factory costs $5,550 (per order) to process, and holding inventory costs $1.25 per unit per week for each unit in the warehouse.

Historical weekly demand data												
Week	1	2	3	4	5	6	7	8	9	10	11	12
Atlanta	33	45	37	38	55	30	18	58	47	37	23	55
Boston	26	35	41	40	46	48	55	18	62	44	30	45
Chicago	44	34	22	55	48	72	62	28	27	95	35	45
Dallas	27	42	35	40	51	64	70	65	55	43	38	47
Los Angeles	32	43	54	40	46	74	40	35	45	38	48	56

In the current distribution system, the cost of transporting a product from the manufacturing facility to a warehouse is given in the second table (see the column "Inbound"). The second table also provides information about transportation cost per unit from each warehouse to the stores in its market area (see the column "Outbound").

Transportation cost per unit product		
Warehouse	Inbound	Outbound
Atlanta	$12.00	$13.00
Boston	$11.50	$13.00
Chicago	$11.00	$13.00
Dallas	$9.00	$13.00
Los Angeles	$7.00	$13.00

Finally, a third table provides information about transportation costs per unit from each existing regional warehouse to all other market areas, assuming this regional warehouse becomes the central warehouse.

Transportation costs per unit with centralized system					
Warehouse	Atlanta	Boston	Chicago	Dallas	Los Angeles
Atlanta	$13.00	$14.00	$14.00	$15.00	$17.00
Boston	$14.00	$13.00	$8.00	$15.00	$17.00
Chicago	$14.00	$8.00	$13.00	$15.00	$16.00
Dallas	$15.00	$15.00	$15.00	$13.00	$8.00
Los Angeles	$17.00	$17.00	$16.00	$8.00	$13.00

Answer the following four questions:

a. A detailed analysis of customer demand in the five market areas reveals that the demand in the five regions are very similar; that is, it is common that if weekly demand in one region is above average, so is the weekly demand in the other regions. How does this observation affect the attractiveness of the new system?

b. Suppose you are to compare the two systems for Product A only, what is your recommendation? To answer this question, you should compare costs and average inventory levels for the two strategies assuming demands occur according to the historical data. Calculate all costs on an annual basis. Also, determine which regional warehouse will be used as the centralized warehouse.

c. It is proposed that in the centralized distribution strategy, that is, the one with a single warehouse, products will be transported from the factory to the warehouse using UPS Ground Service, which guarantees that products will arrive at the warehouse in three days (0.5 week). You do not anticipate any changes in outbound transportation. Of course, in this case, transportation cost for shipping a unit product from a manufacturing facility to the warehouse increases. In fact, in this case, transportation costs increase by 50%. Thus, for instance, shipping one unit from the manufacturing facility to Atlanta will cost $18. Would you recommend using this strategy? Explain your answer.

d. The table below has the key financial accounts for USE. Management believes that this idea for centralizing distribution and using UPS can be applied to 500 items with similar potential savings for each item. The inventory holding cost savings would impact the asset inventory account, setup cost savings would impact the expenses–labor account, and transportation cost savings would impact the expenses–materials account. Estimate the impact that implementing the strategy that you recommend on USE's net income, return on assets, profit margin, and asset turnover.

US Electronics – Key Financial Accounts	
Expenses	**Current ($M)**
Labor	$700.00
Materials	$2,300.00
Overhead	$800.00
Operating Expenses	$3,800.00
Other Expenses	$800.00
Assets	**Current ($M)**
Inventory	$500.00
Receivables	$300.00
Cash	$300.00
Current Assets	$1,100.00
Fixed Assets	$2,900.00
Revenue	**Current ($M)**
Sales Revenue	$5,000.00
Other Revenue	$10.00

Excel Tutorials

DESCRIPTIVE STATISTICS

To access Descriptive Statistics, select DATA → Data Analysis → Descriptive Statistics.

The Input Range is the entire table of information including the column or row labels.

Specify how the data are grouped: by columns or rows.

If Labels are in the first row, select this option.

Specify where the output should go through Output Range, in a New Worksheet, or in a New Workbook.

Select Summary statistics.

Select other options that are desired.

Select OK.

Video Tutorial: http://www.youtube.com/watch?v=Z4n9CfOuaf8

REGRESSION

To access Regression, select DATA → Data Analysis → Regression

Select the Y Range. These are the values that are being predicted.

Select the X Range. These are the values that are used to predict the Y values.

If Labels are in the first row, select this option.

Specify where the output should go through Output Range, in a New Worksheet, or in a New Workbook.

Select other options that are desired.

Select OK.

Video Tutorial: http://www.youtube.com/watch?v=6rOlGbLeQxI

PIVOT TABLES

To start select a cell somewhere in the table to be analyzed.

To access Pivot Tables, select INSERT → Pivot Table

Select a table or range of data (this will default to the table where the cursor was located.

Choose where you want the PivotTable report created, either a New Worksheet or somewhere in the Existing Worksheet.

Select OK.

Select the PivotTable Fields to include in the analysis.

Additional fields can be created by dragging the base data to the VALUES area, right clicking, and selecting Value Field Settings.

Video Tutorial: http://www.youtube.com/watch?v=peNTp5fuKFg

DATA TABLES

Start by setting up a calculation with one or two cells that are changed based on the decision. For example, in an economic order quantity problem, order quantity Q and demand D drive the calculation of the yearly fixed and variable inventory related costs.

Setup a row or column (or both) of input values for the formula.

Just below the first entry of the row, or to the right of the first entry in the column, place a formula that points to the result of the calculation.

Select the cells where the Data Table will perform the calculation. Include the row or column (or both) with the input values for the formula.

Select DATA → What-if Analysis → Data Table

If row data are used, in the Row input cell, insert a reference to where the row values go in the calculation.

If column data are used, in the Column input cell, insert a reference to where the row values go in the calculation.

Select OK.

Video Tutorial: http://www.youtube.com/watch?v=qWLHJ4dDUoo

SOLVER

Start by setting up the problem. The problem needs to have one or more cells that will form the solution to the problem. These are called the Changing Variable Cells. Next, relationships that are dependent on the values in the Changing Variable Cells that define problem Constraints need to be defined. Finally, an Objective cell that captures the cost or profit associated with any solution defined by the values in the Changing Variable Cells needs to be defined.

- Access the Solver by selecting DATA → Solver.
- Set Objective to the Objection function cell.
- Select to Maximize, Minimize, or set the Objective cell to a particular value.
- Add Constraints as appropriate for the problem.
- Select Make Unconstrained Variable Non-Negative if the Changing Variable Cells should not take negative values.
- Select a Solving Method and use Simplex LP whenever all the equations used in the model are linear because this will guarantee an optimal solution. Otherwise experiment with GRG Nonlinear and Evolutionary solvers. These are techniques that will work with non-linear problems and do not guarantee optimal solutions.
- Select Solve.

Video Tutorial: http://www.youtube.com/watch?v=K4QkLA3sT1o

Index